XII

12 WORDS

THAT
CHANGE
EVERYTHING

IAN PRUKNER

ISBN: 978-1-952840-57-9

Cover design:

Manuscript editing & Interior format—UNITED HOUSE Publishing

Interior design: Matt Russell | Marketing Image | marketing-image.com | mrussell@marketing-image.com

Produced in the United States of America

2024—First Edition

CONTENTS

INTRODUCTION - WORDS MATTER 7

I.   OUR WORDS ARE CREATING OUR WORLD 15

II.   TRUTH 25

III. RELEVANCE 39

IV. BELIEF 49

V.   ACTION 59

VI. SYSTEMS: DON'T JUST DO, AUTOMATE 75

VII. ATTITUDE 93

VIII. HEART 109

IX. RELENTLESS 121

X.   CONSISTENCY 135

XI. COMMITMENT 147

XII. FOCUS 157

XIII. FAITH 179

ENDNOTES 189

ABOUT THE AUTHOR 195

RESOURCES 199

WORDS MATTER

… but acting on them matters most. So, let's get that out of the way first.

DID YOU SAY SOMETHING?

In a smoke-filled valley, thick with the smell of gunpowder, you can hear the thunder of the cannons in the distance. The explosions, screams, and smells of war surround you, but you no longer pay attention to them. It's as if you've grown numb to anything but survival. The war has been dragging on for seven years; you wonder if there's any end in sight.

In the early 1780s, many men found themselves inextricably tied to a conflict between the greatest superpower in the world, Great Britain, and her fledgling colonies in America. Arguably, the most important conflict in the history of the civilized world, the American Revolution, began and finished with one word, independence. That word burned in the hearts of the patriots and their commanders as they, a ragtag army of underdogs, took on the greatest military force the world had ever known. It was this one word that gave the Continental Army meaning, purpose, hope, and determination. This one word allowed them to succeed against all odds, birthing the greatest nation mankind has ever known.

Words matter. They hold creative power. They start wars and finish them. They shape our lives in every conceivable way and allow us to shape the lives of those around us. They live deep in the recesses of our souls. The words "I have a dream,"[1] decades after being proclaimed by the great Martin Luther King Jr., still electrify the hearts of all who hear his visionary words. "December 7, 1941—a date which will live in infamy"[2] reminds a nation of incredible resolve. "Give me liberty, or give me death"[3] still embodies the spirit of the great American experiment.

WORDS MATTER. Words allow us to impact the world. They allow our lives to sprawl and live out across the centuries, reaching further than just our lifetimes. They are interwoven in the fabric of our existence, and they give meaning to our human experience. Words alone are uniquely human. Of all the species on earth, there is but one in control of language. Whether spoken, written, signed, or otherwise, words help us to color our world with meaning and vibrance. They move our souls with passion, they call us to great heights, and they comfort us in our lowest lows. They form our representation and record our time on Earth. They give weight to our existence. They instruct and destroy. Words can lift us up, and they can tear us down. They connect us. They can burn with passion or sting with the heartbreak of grief.

Words have been, and continue to be, foundational to our ability to communicate and cooperate as a progressive society.

Our words are literally creating our world. What we speak about, we bring about. Our words not only create but simultaneously give meaning to life. In many ways, we are our words, and they are us. There are 26,900 words in the English language—all unique, all with meaning, and all with place. But, there are some words, when assimilated into our lives and allowed to impart the ideas and truths they represent, that change everything. This book is an exploration of 12 words that changed everything in my life and in the lives of tens of thousands of entrepreneurs and leaders I have had the honor to lead. These 12 words we are about to explore transformed everything about my existence. From unhappy, overweight, and broke, to living an incredibly fulfilling and joyful life, these are the words that not only marked my journey but created and defined it. I believe, if you let them, they will also have a profound and lasting impact on your life. In the following 12 chapters, we will dissect and deep dive into the layers, the nuance, and the power of these 12 words. But before we do, I want to set the stage.

WHY DOES THIS MATTER?

Today, our words are under attack. We have more information and less understanding than ever before. As part of a relentless redefinition campaign, our words, and all that flow from them, are being redefined, reimagined, and stripped of their power. With constant and unrelenting attempts to redefine and reconstruct meaning, the efficacy of our words today is more important than ever. When you strip a word of its meaning, you strip it of its creative and communicative power. When our words no longer carry the ability to define and communicate with power and clarity, we become powerless.

The agreed definition of a word allows us a starting point on which we can build the pillars of communication and cooperation. Imagine a society where $50 means one amount to one party and a drastically different amount to another party. Without an agreed-upon value, one of the parties would surely be upset. When the discrepancy is discovered, all work and progress come to a halt since both sides are unclear as to what value they should be giving and are expecting in return. The same thing happens to our society when our words are not clear and agreed upon. *Are we talking about the same thing?* When our words are ambiguous, one or both of the parties are sure to be met with disappointment. That disappointment slows and eventually halts progress because progress requires cooperation from other people. The heights our society has reached have largely been founded upon the principles of clearly defined communication and cooperation, made possible by our words and their meanings.

There are quite a few examples of redefinition happening right in front of our eyes. Consider the recent example of a United States senator closing the Senate prayer with the customary "amen" followed by an "a-women".[4] The word "amen", in its literal meaning, stands as "so be it", but its context here has been shifted to a gender-specific verb. Or, look at the redefining of the word "tolerance" to mean "blind acceptance and celebration." If you don't accept and espouse this belief or value, then you are intolerant. Maybe we can see it in the re-shaping of the phrase "fact-checking" to mean censorship. Even before these "redefinitions of the month" began, the fabric of our language was already being systematically eroded.

Phrases like "I love you" or "I hate that" are used as commonplace figures of speech. They no longer carry any literal meaning. We are redefining the role of those words and the impact they have in our lives. People who have never experienced the commitment and sacrifice of real love, many times, believe they are *in love*, when, what they are experiencing may really be lust or infatuation. Many misbelieve they are experiencing love, when really, they have no idea what love is. This erroneous belief could lead them to feel that love doesn't work when their relationships fail. Many have defined mere acquaintances, romantic interests, or even physical attraction as love; they mistake love for a feeling. But, anyone who knows real love knows love is a VERB. It's an action. It's also a choice. 1 Corinthians 13: 4-8 (NIV) says: "Love is patient, love is kind. It does not envy, it does not boast, it is not proud, it does not dishonor others, it is not self-seeking, it is not easily angered, it keeps no record of wrongs, love does not delight in evil but rejoices with the truth. It always protects, always trusts, always hopes, always perseveres. Love never fails." We view this passage as one of the most robust and complete definitions of love ever written, and yet, today, love means almost none of those things. Its definition and power is being eroded daily, used, and treated as commonplace.

In the Bible, there is a story about the Tower of Babel (Genesis 11). As the story goes, the human race began gaining great knowledge and wisdom. As their knowledge and wisdom grew, they decided they would build a tower as a monument, to bring glory to themselves and their achievements. This tower was to be the largest tower ever created, reaching all the way to Heaven. The people were so impressed with their engineering and creative ability, they began to worship themselves instead of God. As the Bible depicts it, God, recognizing the capacity of the human spirit and ingenuity, decided to scramble their languages so they would never again be able to communicate and cooperate to build such a monument to themselves.

Here's the key: When God confused their languages, he limited their effectiveness. Imagine, for example, that this book was written in French, but you don't speak French. While the author's meaning may be understood by someone who speaks the language, to a non-French speaking reader, the meaning remains locked, hidden inside, sounds with no meaning. Because we don't understand the meaning, its lessons become lost. What was full of power and instruction now holds neither and has no power to transform us. In the same way, when we redefine or lack a complete understanding of our words, they lose their meaning. A lack of understanding creates a loss of power.

12 WORDS

As I started on the journey of writing this book, it became readily apparent to me it would be impossible to have a meaningful discussion of every powerful and profound word in our language. There are thousands of words and even more ideas communicated by them that could have, or should have, made it into this book. It is precisely for this reason that I debated even writing it. "What about this word?", "What about that one?", "You know, this really should have been in here." 12 words that change everything are sure to draw criticisms and critics who hurl them. And honestly, I must admit, I'm woefully underprepared to take on the task of whittling down the English language into the 12 "right" words. I'm not a linguist or a professor of linguistics. But I have seen, firsthand, the vast and creative power that words hold in our lives.

It's not necessary to know the gear ratios and mechanics of what makes a bike work *before* you actually ride the bike. In fact, you could become a world champion cyclist and have limited knowledge of the actual working of the bike's construction and mechanisms. In the same way, while my expertise in linguistics is limited, my applied knowledge of the words we will discuss in this book is vast. I've lived them. And their power has been unleashed in my life. I've transformed from 35 lbs. overweight, broke, lazy, and unhappy, to living the life of my dreams, and I created that world, first, with my words.

The words that will be discussed within these pages have had a profound impact on my life. I decided to pursue this project because I believe countless lives can experience the change and growth I found by living out the lessons of these powerful words. I'm confident these 12 words will resonate and impact you in many of the ways they have impacted me.

There are entire genres of words this book leaves completely unaddressed. Ideas, like hate, revenge, greed, and the words that embody them, have no doubt shaped the world in significant, and sometimes ugly ways. Words like love, feelings, emotion, and community haven't made their way into the book either. They also have, undoubtedly, molded the world in significant ways. Each of the 12 words that change everything is given their own chapter. Within each chapter, there are associated words and ideas that are inextricably tied to the main idea the chapter unpacks. In the coming pages, I will pour all of my energy into sharing with you the strength, power, lessons, and life held within these 12 words, their impact on my life, and their power to impact yours.

—

CHAPTER 1

OUR WORDS ARE CREATING OUR WORLD

Words have shaped VIRTUALLY all of human history. Since the beginning of time, our words, first shared primarily through oration, gave us the ability to communicate and cooperate. Today, our texts and tweets spread our ideas at the speed of light. Words matter. They have always mattered. As we listen to the speeches of world leaders and read the writings of visionaries, icons, and incredible communicators, we are moved to action. We are challenged to grow beyond our current limits, inspired, or moved to tears. Words, both spoken and written, are deeply ingrained in all aspects of our lives. But, this wasn't always the case.

DID YOU SAY SOMETHING?

The advent of language and the written word have changed the entire trajectory of humanity. For the first several thousand years of history, the human race was completely verbal. All knowledge was required to pass orally from one person to another and from one generation to the next. Progress, as a race, was slow and small in scale, as the total knowledge acquired by humanity was to be re-earned and passed on with every generation. So, much of the wisdom of previous generations, would find itself lost in the sands of time. As written words and symbols became more commonplace, it was possible to record and preserve the learning and knowledge of the generations before. The problem was, when we moved forward, our knowledge, written on the walls of the family cave, did not. The invention of paper coincided with and even created the birth of many great societies. For the first time, instead of leaving all the recorded knowledge behind when forced to relocate, humans now could record knowledge, store it, and transport it efficiently. With the ability to easily record and transport ideas and the words that represent them, human society flourished.

IS IT DARK IN HERE?

We can see this growth phenomenon again by dissecting the time known as the Dark Ages and juxtaposing the subsequent Renaissance period that followed. For roughly 1000 years, there was almost no human progress. This era, commonly referred to as the Dark Ages, lasted for almost a millennia. Although caused by a variety of factors, among the top contributors to this lack of advancement was the almost complete lack of access to the written word. Even though it had existed for thousands of years, access to writings of any sort was virtually non-existent to the mass majority of the population. Direct access to the most advanced thinking, and the writings that expressed those ideas, was extremely limited, found only in the most elite libraries of different world powers. The ability to duplicate and distribute the written word was costly and time-consuming. Many projects dragged on for months, as scribes painstakingly copied one manuscript to the next. The libraries and storehouses that held almost all of the world's knowledge were often the targets of attack during the numerous wars and raids of the time. When manuscripts were lost, stolen, or destroyed, it would take years to locate another copy that scribes could duplicate. This narrow centralization of information led to an almost total stall in human progress. The Dark Ages were marked by the inaccessibility of information, resulting in the lack of progress caused by generations and generations starting over at zero.

It would come as little surprise that the end of the Dark Ages and the beginnings of the Renaissance, an era of accelerated progress in the arts, knowledge, literature, learning, and culture, correlated closely with the invention of the Gutenberg printing press. The Gutenberg project marked the first ability to mass duplicate written volumes for wide-scale distribution. With books like the Gutenberg Bible and the mass production of other classic works, the printing press made literature more readily available to the general population. The press could do in minutes what it took scribes months and years to accomplish. Literacy rates spiked and an inferno of knowledge and learning catapulted the human race into a period of explosive growth. This era, commonly referred to as the Renaissance, was caused, at least in part, by the ability to transfer the best, most accurate, and recent knowledge quickly and inexpensively to mass amounts of the population. No longer dependent on the verbal spread of ideas and the interpretation of those ideas from the storytellers who told them, average people now had direct access to the source. The thinking, ideas, and understanding of the greatest writers, leaders, and historians in the world were now readily available to the average person.

WHEN WE KNOW BETTER, WE DO BETTER

Our newfound distribution capability of the written word brought with it the ability to take the most valuable knowledge and harness the creative power of the law of large numbers. Suddenly, after thousands of years of the written word being rare and centralized, only available to the wealthy and influential, relatively large percentages of humanity are now reading, understanding, and synthesizing. New ideas, methods, and understandings began springing up, pushing the human race aggressively toward a new world. Words hold within them the creative power of progress. Inside them lie the ideas, truths, and principles upon which the greatest of societies can exist.

A THIRD BOOM

Does it seem like the world is speeding up? To me, it seems every passing year is moving faster and faster. Much of that speed is thanks to the creation of the internet. With the advent of the internet, the speed and ease of access to all knowledge of human history has exploded. Today, virtually everyone, everywhere has access to the entire library of human knowledge at their fingertips. This invention is the predictable creator of record growth in technology, connectivity, and progress. Where there is understanding and communication, there is growth, prosperity, and peace.

YOUR LANGUAGE SETS YOUR LIMITS

Words tell an incomparable amount about the person speaking them. The Bible says, "For out of the abundance of the heart the mouth speaks" (Matt. 12:34, ESV). What's on our minds and in our hearts, eventually, leaves the internal world and begins to shape our external one. In other words, what's inside eventually comes out. Our words give life and action to our innermost thoughts, our greatest desires, and our deepest fears. Words bring life to our ideas and change the direction of our lives.

The vast majority of this book will be discovering and describing, in detail, 12 words that can change your life in a predictable yet powerful way. These 12 words will be used to shape your life positively, but before we get to those, we need to address a handful of words that have negative effects on our lives. These words do more to hold us back from

...WHAT'S INSIDE EVENTUALLY COMES OUT.

our potential than almost anything else in the world. They kill more dreams than obstacles, challenges, and setbacks combined. When we speak negatively, we experience negativity. When we verbalize limitations, we become limited. The way we speak and the words we use will either give us wings or put us in chains.

WEAKNESS WORDS

We are going to call these words weakness words. This is because they convey to others, and our subconscious mind, a state of weakness or lack. Weakness words are words that describe a posture of uncertainty and lack. The truth is, there are probably dozens or hundreds of words that could or should be described here, but I'm going to hammer out a few of the most egregious assailants on the human spirit and achievement.

They are the byproduct of non-alignment between our intention and commitment. In other words, what we want and what we're willing to do to get it are not aligned. When we like the idea of something but lack the commitment to execute it, we use weakness words to describe our state. Words like "I'll try," "maybe," and "we'll see" are the epitome of non-commitment verbalized. They express the void between our aspirations and execution and release us from the requirement to follow through. When we speak in weakness, we will live timidly. Weakness words, subconsciously, erode our self-confidence and the confidence others have in us.

Weakness words give us wiggle room. The problem with wiggle room is that we take it. When there's some wiggle room in our clothes, we fill it. When there's some wiggle room on the deadline, we use it. Wiggle room is the enemy of execution. When we use weakness words habitually, we erode our believability, both in ourselves and others. Our subconscious mind gets in the habit of not taking our directions and COMMITMENTS seriously, and before we know it, we can no longer force ourselves to materialize wins because we've gone soft. Winners have a sixth sense, an awareness of, and an almost allergic reaction to the use of these weakness words. When they hear these words and phrases, internally, they know they are dealing with an amateur. Pros speak in certainties. Their words create confidence in others and themselves. Let's take a look at six of the most destructive weakness words here.

1. CAN'T

There's a difference between "can't" and "won't." There are very few things we *can't* do. There are a plethora of things we *won't* do, and *can't* helps us to evade the responsibility of choosing not to do them. We are capable but unwilling to put in the time, effort, energy, or resources to accomplish them. Rather than having to face the hard truth that these things simply

THERE'S A DIFFERENCE BETWEEN "CAN'T" AND "WON'T."

aren't as important to us as we claim, we create a convenient lie: the lie of *can't*. The problem with this is many of us are excusing ourselves of our God-given destinies by crying can't. The truth is, we can, it's just not that important to us. The next time you think you can't, try saying, "It's simply not important to me right now," because that's the truth. We all make time and put forth effort for the things that are important to us. So, the next time you think you can't get to your kid's game, try telling them they're just not as important to you as other priorities. Ouch. The truth is painful, and many times, it's that very pain that allows us to course correct and take care of the most important things in our lives. There's nothing you can't do if you want to bad enough. Literally, all progress is a triumph over can't. Something that couldn't be done before gets done, and progress is made. You *can*. Period.

WHEN WE BELIEVE WE CAN'T, WE DON'T.

The other issue with the word "can't" is that when we repeat it often enough, our subconscious eventually begins to believe it. We tend to approach new challenges and opportunities from the subconscious operating system of "can't." When we believe we can't, we don't. We don't research, we don't attempt, we don't learn, and we don't grow. We don't because we believe we can't. If we remove that word from our vocabulary, we will find our new verbiage actually holds the solution to our problem. Telling your child you've chosen to prioritize a work meeting over their game is something almost none of us would ever say to our child. But it's something we would do to our child over and over and over. The very act of disclosing the truth helps us better prioritize our lives. The fact is, we could do something about that game. We could choose differently if we understand that "can't" is really a choice. When we believe we *can't*, we *don't*, and we shut ourselves off from the solutions that are waiting to enrich our lives.

2. TRY

As the great Yoda says, "Do or do not. There is no try."[5] Trying is lying. It's the word we use to excuse ourselves from having to give our full effort and total commitment. It is also the word we use to erode our self-confidence and others' confidence in us. In this world, you get paid for results, not for effort. Trying is about effort, and doing is about results. I will or I won't. Commit. Don't try, do.

TRYING IS LYING.

3. MAYBE

Maybe it is the proverbial fence-sitting of life. The epitome of non-commitment. The fact is, we have a choice in everything we do or do not do. Great leaders make decisions quickly and definitively and are slow to change them. Followers make decisions slowly and change them almost immediately. Maybe seeks to preserve the status quo and mask our inaction with good intentions. It also shelters us from the pain of saying no. Yet, no is exactly the word that sets us free from the big yeses in our lives. If we can't make routine decisions decisively, how will we make major ones? Maybe also undermines our subconscious ability to take direction. It doesn't know whether we are or aren't, it doesn't know whether we're going or staying, starting or finishing. A subconscious that is confused is a subconscious that is ineffective.

4. BLAME—IT'S NOT MY FAULT

While this is clearly not a single word, it is a phrase that has trapped many people into lives of mediocrity and quiet desperation. The fact is, the state of your health, relationships, and financial stability are all your fault. That can be a tough thing to hear, but the results of this are even tougher to live with. Our results are the byproducts of our thinking, beliefs, and actions. Our life is, quite literally, our fault, good or bad. While we can't control everything happening to us, we can control how we respond. Responsibility is key. When we own where we are in our life, we also own the solution, or at least the potential to solve our issues and create the life we want. But when we blame our current situation on others, we give away our power to change it. When we look for outside solutions to internal challenges, we will stay stuck for extended periods of time. Even when things aren't our fault, we can always ask what we could have done to avoid this or what we can do to better prepare for the next time. When we blame others, we remove ourselves from the temporary pain of taking responsibility, and we lock in the permanent pain of mediocrity.

5. BUSY

Most people are busy going nowhere. Today, being busy is a badge of honor. When you ask someone how they are, it's totally normal to say, "Busy." Busy is all about priorities. As I discussed in my earlier book *Byproduct*,[6] we all have time for what's important to us, and we all have the same 24 hours in a day. Largely, what becomes of our lives is a result of what we choose to do within those 24 hours. So many people fill their lives to the brim with good things; there is little space left for the *great* things. Our goal shouldn't be busyness, but rather, *significance*. It's great you are doing things, but do the things you're doing matter? The most successful people in the world master saying no. They say no to lots of good things, in order to say yes to the best things. A great question that helps me ward off busyness is: *Is this going to get me closer to or further from my goals and dreams?* When I was a pastor, one of the things I would remind the congregation repetitively is, the key ability in God's Kingdom is availability. Are you available for the things that matter most in life?

6. THINK

I *think* so. I need to *think* about it. Let me *think* it over. While thinking is critical, we possess enough instinct and context to make most decisions quickly and accurately. Most people possess the ability to think themselves out of most things. As Tim Grover, CEO of ATTACK Athletics, Inc., says in his book *RELENTLESS: From Good to Great to Unstoppable*[7], "DON'T THINK." Get out of your head and act. A bad decision made on Monday is better than a good one made on Friday. Why? Because by Tuesday or Wednesday, we've realized we made the wrong choice, we've learned from it, and are back on the right path by Thursday, a day ahead of time! High achievers trust themselves and their instincts. Winners know if they make the wrong decision, and they have the capability to correct it quickly, coming out ahead.

CHAPTER 2

TRUTH

truth
/trŏŏTH/

noun
1. the quality or state of being true.
2. that which is true or in accordance with fact or reality.

noun: **the truth**[8]

"The truth is incontrovertible. Malice may attack it, ignorance may deride it, but in the end, there it is."
Winston Churchill[9]

T ruth is the rock on which all other things stand. It has been here since the beginning and will be here long after we're all gone. It is everlasting. It is the foundation of all things. It is the word on which all other words hang. Truth reduces the complexities of a man down to his word. Truth is the foundation and baseline-building block of all society. Truth is the embodiment of the constant. It is accurate, just, and right. It is the truth that holds cause and effect together, the foundation of all justice, and the cornerstone of all cooperation. There is extreme power in truth. When the truth is understood and agreed upon, it creates the foundation for all human achievement and performance. Because we have understood the truths of gravity and lift, people, from all around the planet, can work together, or independently, with that truth as their foundation to continue to create advancements in air and space travel. Without that truth, there would be no foundation on which to build, just many attempts to fly, with no capacity to understand what worked, what didn't, and why. Truth has always and will always exist. It is constant and unchanging, but understanding it is not enough. It's not sufficient for the truth to simply exist. It must be known and then applied. Gravity and lift have always existed on our planet. Yet, for most of history, nobody understood them. It wasn't until very recently, in the scale of human history, that anyone attempted to harness them. To understand and act upon those truths was to create the marvel of flight.

Time and money would be wasted and lives lost, in droves, as people, well-intentioned but ignorant of the forces of gravity and lift, try to build aircraft while not taking those forces into account. There is power in truth because it provides a platform from which we can build our lives. It's a solid rock, an unwavering constant, immune to the whims of public opinion that we can use as a compass, a direction of true north. Truth is rooted in the universal principles that govern the world, and it is the currency of trust. It is a true north that, no matter our differences of perspective and opinion, is ultimately a relied upon standard. Why does this matter? It matters because your level of success currently, and your ability to repeat it, depends on how deeply rooted your truth belief systems are. False beliefs create false outcomes.

Can anyone know the truth? In short, yes. Truth is known by its fruit and tested against time. Today, those who love falsehoods regularly attack the concept of truth. They make arguments that truth is both relative and personal. In other words, what's true for you may not necessarily be true for me. What they are referring to is not truth but perspective or experience. Truth is not situational; it is eternal. It's not true sometimes or for some people, but it's true all of the time and for all people. It is larger than both our experience and our perspective, which are both limited by the flicker of time we call a lifetime. Our perspective and experience are limited, first and foremost, by us. We are limited by our capacity to understand and contain truth. Imagine somebody holding a gallon of water and thinking it contains all of the water that exists in the world. That's exactly what many people do with truth. They have the capacity to contain a gallon's worth of truth, while the world is filled with oceans of truth that they have not contained. Just because we don't have the capacity to receive it, understand it, or contain it doesn't mean that it doesn't exist. It just means we're limited in our experience with it.

People love to say things like, "There is no absolute truth." Ironically, if that were true, this statement itself would become an absolute truth. Stagnation thrives off of ignorance and fear, which are the byproducts of a lack of truth. Independence and progress thrive off of high-truth environments. Here's a truth: human beings are capable of learning and improving. This is a fact, that being understood allows one to keep progressing, even when met with initially undesirable outcomes. The belief that when we get better, it gets better, allows us to make progress in our lives amidst opposition. The idea that if you apply yourself long enough and consistently enough, in a given direction, you can become successful, allows us to choose the outcomes of our lives. The lie that success is about luck or talent creates adverse action, one where we don't see the value in trying to improve our skill sets. In my book, *Byproduct*, I outline the idea that thoughts create beliefs, beliefs create actions, and actions, ultimately, create our results. They are all byproducts of the step before. When our thinking is truth based and accurate, we form truth-centered belief systems. In turn, we take truth-centered actions and create predictable, positive outcomes. The same is true in the opposite direction. If our thoughts are incorrect and not based on truth, we take faulty actions and end up with negative outcomes.

RELATIVITY

There is a movement today to discredit truth by claiming it is relative; what is true for me may not be true for you. Truth is not relative, it is final and authoritative. If something appears to be true for one person and not true for another, it means we're only seeing a piece of the whole puzzle; a micro variation inside of the system of a macro truth. It is possible for us to have varying experiences with the same truth based on our experience and perspective. It's also possible for us to have varying beliefs about what those experiences represent. So, how do we account for relativity? The answer is simple: perspective and experience. Limited perspective and experience allow us only a glimpse at the total truth. In other words, from our line of sight, something might look true in one instance and false in another iteration of that instance. Most truths are large and occupy large spaces and time.

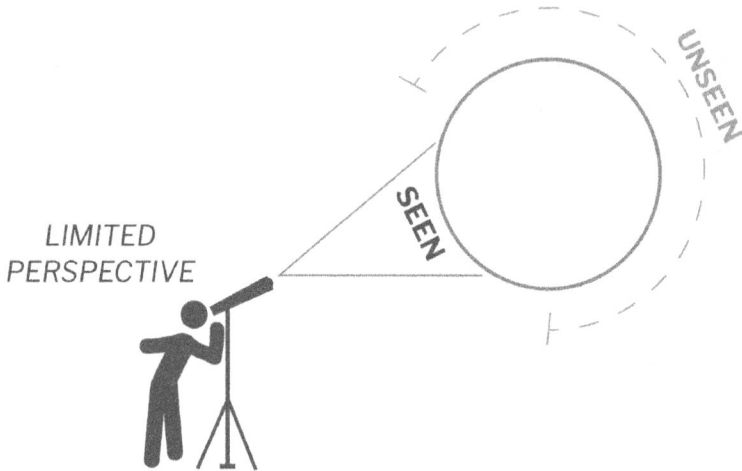

If we refer to the graphic above, we see truth as a complete sphere, and our limited perspective only allows us to view a piece of that sphere. To the person viewing from the right side, everything in their life is filtered through the right-side truth paradigm. In graphic B, the same truth is being viewed from the opposite vantage point. This person filters all of their experience and interactions through a left-side truth paradigm. It is important to understand that just because our ability to perceive the truth is limited by our perspective, doesn't mean it doesn't exist. It simply means our capacity is not large enough to partake in its totality.

Our own personal experiences are also often culprits of clouding the truth. Think about somebody who has played a lot of slot machines in Vegas but never won. They may conclude, based on their experience, you can't win at slot machines in Vegas. While the experience may have been accurate for them, it is not true. There are lots of people who win enormous amounts of money at slot machines in Vegas. Just because our experience hasn't validated it, doesn't mean that it's invalid.

Our experience is also dependent on our ability to connect the dots between cause and effect. We may experience a truth but be unable to comprehend it or benefit from it because of our lack of ability to understand cause and effect. A couple of months ago, my 14-year-old daughter failed one of her exams. She was so upset and heartbroken about it because that failed exam meant she wouldn't be eligible to play in the remainder of her high school basketball season. When asked what she learned about the experience, she replied that the test was unfair. Then, she went on about how other kids had failed, and it wasn't just her, and a litany of other reasons, in her mind, that she hadn't passed the exam. The truth she missed, unfortunately, was that she simply had not prepared well enough. Rather than blaming it on the test, other people, or circumstances, none of which would help her pass that test again in the future, understanding the actual cause of the failure and correcting it would have been valuable. After listening to her laundry list of potential causes for the failure, I asked her a simple question, "Did anyone in your class pass the exam?" She replied that several had. If others were able to pass the exam, then the exam could not have been the problem or nobody would have passed it. As I helped walk her through that reality and addressed some of her other concerns, the truth became readily apparent. What was the difference between the kids who had passed that exam and the kids who did not? Preparation. They had prepared more adequately than the kids that had failed the exam.

As simple as it sounds, there are many people living in experiences similar to what I've just described that never draw the correct line between cause and effect. They spend their entire lives trying to fix problems that were never the problem to begin with. Furthermore, not all cause-and-effect truth relationships are immediate. For example, eating high-fat burgers every day for 30 years will probably give you heart disease. Eating a burger today will probably not give you heart disease today. Our limited experience and perspective show us only one piece of total truth that stands alone and may not represent the entire truth.

Think about it this way, imagine you are standing at the front of a large lecture hall with a whiteboard stretching from one end to the other. It is over 30 feet long. Imagine you are standing two feet away from that blackboard. Your perspective would only allow you to take in a piece of the equation. You may be able to make sense of the piece of the equation you can see. However, the piece you can see, your perspective, or your experience, is not representative of the whole. Only as you back away from the whiteboard, does more and more of the equation come into view. When you stand at the back of the classroom, you can view the entire equation in its totality. In this example, the equation represents the truth. The limited perspective and experience with the equation represent our interaction with a larger truth. The larger and more robust our experiences and perspectives can become, and the longer view of time we can filter those through, the more likely it is we are able to discover the truth.

Perspective: The ability to see and understand things from multiple points of view.

Because our filter point of interaction with the truth is our perspective, it merits discussing it in more detail here. What we lack most, today, is perspective. So many of our world's problems would disappear immediately if we could just bring ourselves to see from other people's points of view. It is the human condition to be primarily self-interested, and the leader's condition to see and understand a variety of interests.

Imagine for a second this graphic.

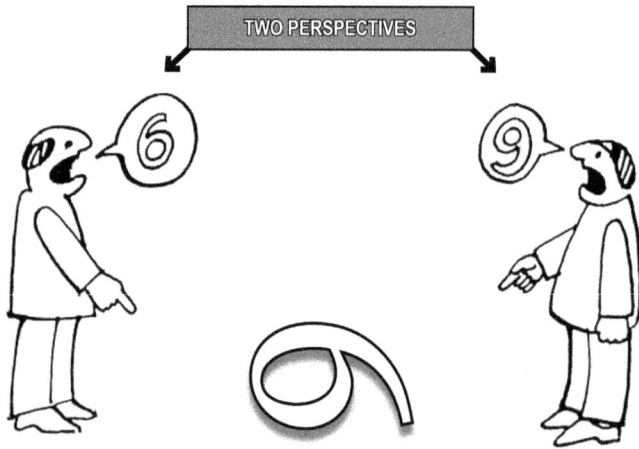

Here, two strangers are arguing about whether the number represented is a six or a nine. To each, their point of view reassures them of their correctness. However, as you can see from afar, both appear to be right. This is how much of the world works. Our limited perspective allows us to feel very certain we are right and others are wrong. They feel much the same way and not much gets accomplished. Perspective allows you to see from not just your point of view but also others' points of view. Perspective makes you powerful because it allows you to understand what other people see and how other people think. Seeing what's important to them and the things that they value, makes you a master negotiator. It allows you to find common ground and create cooperative spaces with almost anybody, at any time. Perspective allows us to play above the grid. In the same example, not only are we able to understand and empathize with the other person's point of view, but we can ask better questions. We can, in this case, look for some context. Are there other clues that will help us see the truth? Remember, people always act on their beliefs. Their beliefs, in large part, are formed by their perspectives. If we can understand their perspective, we can accurately predict patterns of behavior. Even in the art of persuasion, understanding others' perspectives and what those perspectives cause them to value, can help identify areas to create win-wins that otherwise would not be understood.

Now, take a look at this example: It's the same image as before, but it's now in the context we can clearly see this is a nine. But, we can only see this by rising above our own limited perspective and looking for a larger, well-rounded perspective. Is it possible we're not seeing the complete picture? With more perspective and more information, we have more wisdom. When we have more wisdom, we make better choices and take better actions. It's easier to dig into your position and character-assassinate people who don't see things like you. But, a leader looks for common ground and challenges their own perspective in a quest for what is right. Perspective in leadership is everything for the long-term sustainability and viability of any endeavor.

DECISION-MAKING

Our ability to recognize and act on truth determines the quality of our decisions. We usually make the best decisions we can with the best information we have.

Virtually all of our decision-making is clouded. The culprit of that clouding is the lens of our own perspective. Our inability to see other sides, interests, fears, wins, and losses inhibits us from making truly sound decisions on a regular basis. Perspective impacts every area of decision-making, whether at home, with our health, or in business.

One thing driving so many would-be leaders from success is their failure to recognize, respect, and react to the human condition. The human condition is the tendency for people to do things in their own self-interest. Knowing this allows you to start every conversation, negotiation, or hire understanding that the person sitting across from you is primarily self-interested. What do they want? What motivates them?

Instead of starting every conversation with our own wants and needs, which are good, instead, we can start those same meetings with a different perspective: What do they want? How can I meet that need and look for opportunities others may miss by being too self-interested?

Perspective is often shaped by personality. While all people and personalities are different, there are personality types, tendencies, and traits that lead to common perspectives. By understanding different personality types, we can also understand their accompanying perspectives. When we understand this, we can understand how people are likely to view and interact with the truth. This gives us great power in being able to help ourselves, and the people around us, achieve the results we desire in life. Because personality shapes perspective so greatly, and perspective shapes interaction with truth so greatly, a discussion about basic personality types is warranted here. In any family or organization, there are essentially five main types of people we are going to encounter. Let's take a few minutes to understand them now.

PERSONALITY TYPES:

THE GOOD-NATURED

The good-natured are fun to have around. They tell the greatest stories, are the life of the party, have a great attitude, and are quick to say yes. They are the first to volunteer and are the organization's cheerleaders. These people often have their perspective clouded by optimism. They tend to think the situation they are in is better than it really is. They underestimate the pitfalls, challenges, and threats. While pleasant to have around, they often make poor long-term choices because they fail to see things clearly. These are the people who tell you a plan will work, even when it won't, because they just don't think critically enough to challenge their optimistic perspective. Have you ever found yourself halfway down a path you were certain would work, only to meet with failure that surprised you? You may be good-natured.

CYNIC

The cynic has heard it all before and doubts everything that anybody says. They create ulterior motives where none exist; they're constantly looking for the rub or the "real reason" something is happening. These people tend to create distrust inside a family or team, especially among leaders. They're always waiting for the other shoe to drop, and they can never take things at face value. Cynics can be valuable because they'll often be the first ones to pick up on the scent of a real issue. The key here is to take the cynic's advice with a grain of salt. They tend to overreact, over-emotionalize, and over complicate the situation.

VICTIM

The victim is different from a cynic in this way: the cynic thinks the system is rigged, and the victim thinks it's rigged *against them*. Specifically, they never have a fair shake or a fair shot. They believe, erroneously, that things are happening *to them*, not because of them. They're quick to tell you what's wrong with the church, or dinner, the sales process, the commission structure, their boss, their subordinates, and the world at large. They'll have you thinking things are far harder than they really are. People with a victim mentality will gladly trade you their power and autonomy for attention and affirmation of their claims.

THE BRAIN

The brain is a valuable member of any team. They problem-solve and constantly look to make improvements. They're very good at what they do but often have a problem integrating their knowledge, resources, or departmental projects into the greater scheme of the team or family unit. These are people who will vehemently argue for their own or departmental interests without considering how the interests of other people are affected. They lack pragmaticism. If decision-making is left in The Brain's hands, certain areas will become ultra-proficient and others completely neglected. They don't have the ability to see the inner workings from 30,000 feet. They tend to be great middle managers but poor executive-level leaders.

THE LEADER

The leader sees, with clarity, all of the competing interests and viewpoints. They are able to organize and conduct the varying people types into productive action. They're able to synthesize the information they see from different perspectives to create the most accurate view of the situation, person, deal, etc. They don't get over-emotionally charged. They give people the benefit of the doubt while learning to judge people by their actions.

Perspective, ultimately, gives us the ability to understand people, data, feedback, and truth. "In God we trust"; all others must have

"IN GOD WE TRUST"; ALL OTHERS MUST HAVE DATA.

data. Even data, when taken out of context, can become a con-text. Perspective allows us to view the world around us and our place in it accurately. Perspective allows us to see through the story or the narrative and see the truth. It helps us make accurate personal decisions. For example, a team member misses a staff meeting. After inquiring, we find they didn't come in to work at all. The next day, the exact same thing happens with a different employee. After missing the staff meeting, and upon inquiry, we realize the employee isn't at work at all. Two unexcused absences, by two different people. How do we respond? The same? The offense is the same. They missed the same amount of time. How should this be addressed? How should the correction be administered? The answer is, it depends. One employee hasn't missed a day of work in the last 7 years. They are always on time and have stellar performance reports. The other employee missed 2 days last month in the same manner. They have already received a warning about their attendance. Perspective allows us to see the nuance, the gray in black and white. And it allows us to make better decisions more quickly, most of the time. It is true that they both missed the meeting. It is also true that they have very different histories of that behavior. Perspective allows us to see the bigger truth and make the right choice more often.

HOW DO WE DEVELOP PERSPECTIVE?

1. through widening our experience base

2. learn from the wisdom and experiences of others

We widen our experience base by purposely seeking out different environments and information than that which we usually surround ourselves with. Going to new places, meeting new people, trying new foods, and engaging in new interactions, help us to broaden our limited perspective base.

Learning from others can take the form of consuming new material. Learning from great leaders is instrumental in condensing time frames when it comes to developing perspective. When we only gain perspective through our own experiences, the process of perspective expansion can take a lifetime. But, through the power of books, audio, and seminars, we can gain others' perspectives, hard-earned over a lifetime of experience, and condense those lessons down into a few minutes or hours. Leadership, in every area of life, requires a wide and far-ranging perspective and viewpoint, unattainable in one's own short lifespan on earth. Wisdom and knowledge, compiled and condensed by others, are absolutely essential. We must seek out mentors and material on purpose with the purpose of seeking new perspectives and gaining wisdom. And, here's the hard part, we must be willing to abandon our viewpoints and beliefs when they contradict the truth

WE MUST BE WILLING TO ABANDON OUR VIEWPOINTS AND BELIEFS WHEN THEY CONTRADICT THE TRUTH

or when it becomes evident our perspectives are no longer serving us. The truth is all around us. It's always been there and will always be there. Our mission in life is to discover it and act on it while eliminating the perspectives that hold us back from living a truth-filled powerful life. Every breakthrough in your health, your marriage, or your finances will be the byproduct of a truth newly found, newly seen, or newly acted on. The truth awaits!

CHAPTER 3

RELEVANCE

rel·e·vance

/ˈreləv(ə)ns/

noun

1. relation to the matter at hand

2. practical and especially social applicability[10]

———

Relevance—To be irrelevant is to be forgotten

The world is changing, and so must we. Relevance has never been more important and, simultaneously, hard to achieve. Relevance is influence in real-time. It's the idea that what you have learned, the value you provide, your brand, or your team doesn't just matter, but it matters now, to me, where I am. Blockbuster is irrelevant. MySpace and Sears, irrelevant. Toys R' Us … Sad, but irrelevant. It's not

> **THE WORLD IS CHANGING, AND SO MUST WE.**

enough to have success; one must be constantly reinventing and reimagining what success and significance may look like in the lives of our consumers. Relevance requires us to look ahead, anticipate, and imagine what it might look like 1, 3, 5, 10, and 50 years from now. The reason I chose to include the word *relevance* here is that innovation, inspiration, imagination, and, quite frankly, all progress, are byproducts of relevance. Relevance forces us not to rest on the laurels of our previous successes. It forces us not to grow complacent in our businesses, skills, and learning. Many people *used* to be somebody. They are masters at work and have a skill set that no longer exists. Irrelevant people find it difficult to compete and succeed in today's world. Their education

RELEVANCE IS INFLUENCE IN REAL-TIME.

and skills have become obsolete. If you think about it, virtually all the skills and knowledge used in daily work life, one hundred years ago, are now irrelevant. And one hundred years from now, the majority of our skills, knowledge, companies, and industries will be irrelevant too. We are all in a never-ending battle against impending irrelevance. Relevance forces growth, and growth forces innovation and progress. From warfare to consumer goods to technologies and clothing styles, everything dates and ages. As it ages, it has less and less influence on culture.

MOVE

When we stay static, we are unconsciously moving toward insignificance and away from relevance. The law of entropy states that everything tends toward disorder. Likewise, everything that is relevant now, over time, trends toward irrelevance. Irrelevance is the direction we naturally head as our comfort and complacency lull our creative capacities to sleep. Leadership, action, and innovation are the forces that allow us to war against that impending irrelevance.

ONE OF THE GREATEST ENEMIES OF RELEVANCE IS SUCCESS.

Success doesn't make us invincible; it makes us fat and lazy. Maybe not physically, but it sure does mentally and emotionally. The grind and scrappiness that got us to the top disappears into the thin air of the summit. The passion, care, and creativity we showed up to our marriage with tend to vanish as the decades go by. Yeah, we got the girl or the guy, but will we keep them? And will we get them over and over and over again, as we continue to pursue them with the vigor and excellence we once did? While we are basking in yesterday's win, someone else is already defining tomorrow. Relevance today comes from a series of wins. Relevance tomorrow comes from playing above the field, seeing where the game is moving, and taking it there.

Look at companies like Blockbuster whose success blinded them from seeing the changing times and technologies that ended up, ultimately, being its demise. The greatest

SUCCESS DOESN'T MAKE US INVINCIBLE; IT MAKES US FAT AND LAZY.

leaders and organizations, the greatest spouses and parents, war against irrelevance with weapons of vision and growth. Staying the same is simply not to be tolerated if we are to remain relevant. The minute we believe we already know that we are good enough, or that we don't need to keep learning, is the moment irrelevance overcomes us. It may not manifest itself for months, years, or even decades, but it is, at that moment, that irrelevance wins.

8 KEYS TO RELEVANCE

Understand this: Relevance is created and cultured. It is on purpose; it is not automatic.

1. PROGRESS

As leaders, we must know, demonstrate, and model progress as a lifestyle. We must understand we don't, as leaders, companies, and influencers, become or stay relevant without progress. The hunger for an organizational culture of continuous learning and improvement is one of the few safeguards against irrelevance. The vision that continuously stretches what is possible allows us to stay at the top of the game. To not get stuck in our ways, in what worked yesterday, in how we've always done it, and to keep forging new paths, new ideas, and new processes, allows us to stay on the right side of the relevancy curve. By definition, relevance requires significance. That current significance must travel and transform with us to remain relevant. Relevance never stays put; it's always moving, so if we're not moving with it, we won't be relevant for long.

2. ANTICIPATE

Leaders understand that with a changing world comes changing and unprecedented opportunities. You are winning where you are? Fantastic. If you don't grow, adapt, and innovate you won't be for long! Where are the next moves? How do we get there? When do we let go of what worked in the past but has run its course? These are the questions that relevant leaders and teams are asking. We must answer them early, and execute them like a savage. When the competition is wondering what happened, we are creating what happened.

Outstanding leaders, teams, and organizations are constantly anticipating, reimagining, and reinventing. They are fixing what's not broken because it is broken, just not yet. It will be broken 20 years from now. Great leaders don't wait for their apparatus to break; they break it on purpose and reconstruct it into something new, beautiful, and world-changing. By the time most companies are just catching up with the latest trend or technological change, it's already obsolete.

RELEVANT ORGANIZATIONS EMBRACE CHANGE QUICKLY.

Relevant organizations embrace change quickly. The key word there is *embrace*. Eventually, change is forced on everyone. Those who stay relevant embrace it and anticipate it instead of fighting it. Instead of wishing for the good old days, relevant groups know that these days are the good old days. And tomorrow will be better. They don't view change as a threat to their way of life but understand that change *is* a way of life. Most people spend more effort fighting change than it would take to implement it. Great leaders see change as not only necessary but a tool for growth. They know that with every change comes the elimination of previous competitors that were unwilling or unable to adapt, as well as new competitors. They don't fear it, they EXPECT it, EMBRACE it, and even CREATE it.

3. DEPLOY

Great teams not only expect and embrace change, but they also create and deploy it. It's not enough to be aware of the next new frontier, but to be relevant, you have to be doing something with it. Relevant organizations understand that deployment is everything. They don't wait for everything to be perfect to bring the product to market (in some industries, like aviation, medicine, etc., this is not the case). They deploy, test, try, and reimagine in a constant never-ending circle, forcing progress as they go. Think of the iPhone, for example. If you are anything like me, you have a host of late-model iPhones strewn about that become kid phones and backup phones. Apple didn't wait until they had the technology to release the iPhone 14 before they went to market. They released iPhone 1, then 2, and then 3. With every new release, they made improvements, went to market, and then continued that process. If you are waiting for everything to be perfect before you deploy, you have already missed your opportunity. Somebody else, somewhere else, has taken the chance and brought that product, idea, service, app, or church to market. Today, it's about speed to market. Get it out there, hunt down feedback from the marketplace, and make improvements.

4. CREATE

Relevant companies and leaders are on the razor's edge of the times. It's not enough to be with the pack. To stay relevant into the future, you must lead the pack. Relevant leaders imagine new and better ways to deliver their products, service, or message. They are constantly dreaming about new profits, new services, and new messages. While most people are yearning for the way it was, relevant leaders are creating the way it will be. Very simply, relevant creators define the future.

> **WHILE MOST PEOPLE ARE YEARNING FOR THE WAY IT WAS, RELEVANT LEADERS ARE CREATING THE WAY IT WILL BE.**

5. YOUNG AT HEART

Age is only a number. As leaders and organizations age, they tend to slow down, become more bureaucratic, and stuck in their ways. History is important. Principles are important. But the ways in which we communicate and deliver that history and those principles are fluid. It's ever-changing. Organizations and leaders who want to be relevant and stay relevant need to stay organizationally young at heart and in mind. Not physically younger, none of us can make that happen, but rather creating young as a way of being, constantly learning, willing to take risks, open to new ideas and technology, and embracing the value of change.

6. DITCH THE WAR STORIES

War stories are important to any team, family, or warrior. They help shape the culture and value systems of organizations. But as leaders, whenever our time, attention, and passion get fixated on the victories of the past, and off of future victories, we are in trouble. It's great to have war stories about what we did and how it was, but most importantly, we need to be creating new victories and new war stories that our people can experience and live firsthand. The demise of almost every brilliant company, leader, family, or organization begins with getting past-focused instead of future-focused. Without having a great battle to fight, the army is useless. As leaders, we must always have a new battle ahead of us. When we battle for something new, we aren't in danger of fighting yesterday's war again and again. We can't get stuck at "I was this and that. Look at what I accomplished 10 years ago." We need to be taking new ground, winning new victories, and leading new conquests. Fading stars talk about what they did; rising stars talk about what they are going to do.

> **WHENEVER OUR TIME, ATTENTION, AND PASSION GET FIXATED ON THE VICTORIES OF THE PAST, AND OFF OF FUTURE VICTORIES, WE ARE IN TROUBLE.**

7. BE EXCELLENT

Don't overthink it, just be great. Excellence is a prerequisite to relevance. Being average doesn't sell. Nobody cares about mediocrity. You don't chase relevance or decide you need to be relevant, you *are* relevant. Be great and keep getting better.

Whatever you do and whoever you are, rest assured, anything you do well will make room for you. Our greatest fear shouldn't be of failure but rather of succeeding at something that doesn't matter. There is a shortage of great people out there. People

> **FADING STARS TALK ABOUT WHAT THEY DID; RISING STARS TALK ABOUT WHAT THEY ARE GOING TO DO.**

expect moderate service, at moderate quality, with moderate speed. Be excellent and you have no choice but to stand out. At the time of writing this book, Amazon is taking over the e-commerce world. One day, this will likely no longer be true, but right now, it's a fact. Why? Excellence. When everyone else ships within 3-5 days, at your cost, Amazon guarantees it to you the next day, sometimes even the same day. They are excellent at delivering the customer experience. Think now about a county renaissance festival, where people come dressed in medieval attire, eat giant turkey legs, and do otherwise strange things. Think about the guy who uses the sticks to twirl about the centerpiece. He does spins and tricks and throws, and even though the slappy sticks mean nothing to the outcome of your life, even though there is absolutely no real-world use for this skill, at that moment, the slappy stick juggler captivates you. He draws you in with his slaps of wizardry. After parting with $50 for your own set of slappy sticks and failing to keep the centerpiece off the ground for even 10 seconds, you realize his excellence made him relevant and drew you in to part with your money. Excellence will always be relevant.

> **BE EXCELLENT AND YOU HAVE NO CHOICE BUT TO STAND OUT.**

8. REINVENT—CHANGE OR DIE

The most relevant companies and people in the world are masters of reinvention. They are chameleons of their time, and sometimes ahead of it, shaping, shifting, and restructuring, as life and trends demand. They escape the pigeonhole of their former greatness as they transform and transcend industries and categorization. Success isn't always permanent. Apple is no longer primarily in the desktop computer business. Will Smith is not primarily the Fresh Prince. 50 Cent is no longer the gangster rapper. They are masters at reinvention. As masters of reinvention ourselves, we've got to constantly look at the horizon for the next iteration of ourselves. Ultimately, who and what we are today is not who and what we will be tomorrow. When we blindly hold on to the past or the present, we sacrifice the future. The problem with that is we're going to live a lot more time in the future than we are going to live today. We must stay relevant to stay significant

CHAPTER 4

BELIEF

be·lief
/bəˈlēf/

noun

1. a state or habit of mind in which trust or confidence is
placed in some person or thing, an acceptance that
a statement is true or that something exists.

2. something that is accepted, considered to be true or held
as an opinion, trust, faith, or confidence in someone or something.[11]

———

You're not beaten until you no longer believe.

Belief shapes every action in our life. It is belief that causes us to move. Belief in an outcome forms and focuses our actions. If we believe we can win, we compete. If we believe it will be worth it, we endure. If we believe we are beaten, we are defeated before we begin. Belief is the emotional anchor to our thoughts. It creates a constructive or destructive view of how we see the world. Beliefs form our working understanding of cause and effect. Our beliefs provide the

YOU'RE NOT BEATEN UNTIL YOU NO LONGER BELIEVE.

framework for understanding our lives and the events in them. They help assign meaning and value to the world around us and create the coloring of the glasses through which we view the world.

We always act on belief. As I discussed in my earlier book, *Byproduct*, beliefs create action. All action in our life is created by or supported by our belief systems. For example, if we heard a fire alarm going off in our college dorm, saw a number of other people running for the stairs, and believed that our building was on fire, we would probably exit the premises as well. Even though, in actuality, there may not be a fire, we believe there is, and so we act accordingly. This is how virtually every action in our life is shaped. Now, let's assume the fire alarm we just discussed was a false alarm and there was no fire. The fact that the fire did not exist did not stop us from taking action as if it did. How many people are taking actions in their life based on things they believe to be true but aren't? One key point to understand here is that action is based on belief, but beliefs do not need to be true to be acted upon. When we act on inaccurate beliefs, we get inaccurate results. If our actions are created by our beliefs, then our beliefs hold the power not only to make us act but to change our actions. When we change our beliefs, we change our subsequent actions and, ultimately, our results.

Beliefs are the syndicate of related thoughts that combine to create a spiderweb of interpretation. They give us meaning and understanding of the world. When we have false or limiting beliefs, we hold as truth that which is not true.

This syndicate of thoughts resides primarily at the subconscious level: Here, there is little care for whether the belief is true or false. The subconscious is not interested in truth; that is an exercise for the conscious mind to engage in and filter out. Once at the subconscious level, the belief is accepted as true and creates the fabric of our subconscious operating system. It is thought around 90% of the decisions we make daily are made at the subconscious level,[12] originating autonomously from the belief system held there. As we proceed, we will examine a number of limiting, erroneous, and empowering beliefs that shape our actions, and ultimately our fixtures. Before we do, I have a question for you. Actually, I have several questions. What do you believe? Why do you believe it? Are your beliefs accurate? How do you know? Are your beliefs serving you? Are your beliefs serving the world around you? To answer these questions gives you great power amongst your peers, most of whom don't know what they believe or why they believe it.

The problem with belief—What we believe, we become.

CONFIRMATION BIAS

Confirmation bias is when we tend to see what we are looking for. Confirmation bias allows our brain to filter out that which appears to be irrelevant or contradictory to our current beliefs and identify and recognize and reinforce stimuli that support it. It effectively allows us to be blind to data that doesn't support our current hypothesis. Confirmation bias is both incredible and dangerous because it limits our ability to see information that contradicts our current belief systems. If your beliefs are serving you, your confirmation bias helps you to stay focused in that lane of belief. If your beliefs aren't serving you, confirmation bias keeps you stuck, trapped in a belief system that appears to validate itself but is incorrect.

FALSE BELIEFS

Beliefs don't need to be true to be believed. There are many people who believe vehemently in falsehoods. Think flat earthers. They believe, contrary to all scientific evidence, that the earth is flat. There are still people who believe that some races of human beings are superior to others. There are many who suffer from a plethora of irrational phobias or beliefs that something poses a larger threat or danger than it actually does. Beliefs are powerful, and inaccurate beliefs hold great power to disrupt and destroy our lives. Many people in sales and business give up when they could be great because of what they believe their friends and family think about them when, in reality, those people aren't thinking about them at all.

BELIEFS DON'T NEED TO BE TRUE TO BE BELIEVED.

LIMITED BELIEFS

Limited beliefs are different from false beliefs in that they may be partially accurate, which is why they are oftentimes hard to recognize. They can be based on fact but not in truth. A great example of a limiting belief would be: "I'm not good at sales." While that may be a fact currently, it doesn't have to remain that way. This is a belief that limits us from our actual potential. Instead of an understanding that if we were to invest time, effort, energy, and resources into learning the skill of sales we would improve. It lures us into believing we just aren't any good at it. Limiting beliefs are dangerous because they are cloaked in truth. It is said that the best lies are the ones wrapped in truth.

LIMITING BELIEFS ARE DANGEROUS BECAUSE THEY ARE CLOAKED IN TRUTH.

Likewise, the most limiting of beliefs are the ones wrapped in facts that are subject to change. We must make certain we do not treat our limiting beliefs as absolutes because they are totally and completely changeable. They may be true right now, but they don't have to remain that way.

NEGATIVE BELIEFS

Negative beliefs are faith in the worst outcome. All of us, to some extent, experience a negativity bias, fear, or worry of the worst-case scenario. Negative beliefs move beyond fear and worry and begin creating actions that move us towards those outcomes, like a negative self-fulfilling prophecy. The Bible says it this way: "For the thing that I fear comes upon me, and what I dread befalls me" (Job 25, ESV). It's statistically proven that most of what you worry about never actually happens. So, when we experience chronic negative beliefs, our best-case scenario is we never actually experience those outcomes, but they steal our joy and peace in the present. The worst-case scenario is that we actually induce and attract the very thing that we fear into our reality. It's fine to be a realist, to count the cost, and to understand the potential risks of any endeavor, but when we inordinately focus on them, it doesn't remove them or reduce them.

IT'S STATISTICALLY PROVEN THAT MOST OF WHAT YOU WORRY ABOUT NEVER ACTUALLY HAPPENS.

AN ATTITUDE OF GRATITUDE WILL ALWAYS BE THE BEST ATTITUDE

Beliefs have consequences. One of the best beliefs you can develop is that things are happening *for you* and not *to you*. When you hold this belief, it's easy to operate with an attitude of gratitude. Gratitude is the byproduct of right believing. When we have a thankful heart, we attract more things to be thankful for.

There are a lot of successful, miserable people out there. That misery could be alleviated with a simple change in

BELIEFS HAVE CONSEQUENCES.

perspective; a gratitude shift. At any given time, there are going to be positive and negative things happening around us. Those two forces always coexist in our lives. It's the perspective with which we view life that sets the tone in our lives. Our perspectives are generally byproducts of our belief systems. Are we going to view life as mostly negative or mostly positive? There are facts to support either worldview. It's up to us to choose the view of the world that is both accurate and beneficial. Just because negative things are happening around us doesn't mean we need to let them have an effect on us. A gratitude shift is learning to be thankful in all things and for all things.

GRATEFUL FOR ALL THINGS

Gratitude is the seed that produces the harvest of happiness. It's easy to get caught up in all the things that aren't quite right, to fixate on the obstacles and the setbacks, and to view them as negative, impeding us from what we think we need to have, be, or have lined up to accomplish our dreams. A gratitude shift is learning to view these things from another perspective; one that says ALL things are working together for our good. The Bible says all things are working for your good (Rom. 8:28, ESV). Notice it says ALL things. Not just some things, not just the things we like, understand, or are easy,

GRATITUDE IS THE SEED THAT PRODUCES THE HARVEST OF HAPPINESS.

but *all* things. If that is the case, then there is reason to be grateful all of the time, no matter our circumstances or surroundings. God's plan for your life is this:

You win! If at the present moment, you aren't winning, maybe you're reading this, and you find yourself in a struggle, know this:

1. There's a reason for the season you are experiencing, and

2. This will be used for your benefit.

In my years of leading people, what I've found is that virtually every struggle, obstacle, and trial is endowed with the seed of equal or greater opportunity. Will your belief system allow you to see this? Within these trials also lies one of three things that the trial needs to import to us.

1. TESTING

In life, it's lesson repeated until lesson is learned. God will not give us more than we can handle, and He definitely won't give us something that will destroy us. Think about it like this—he who is faithful with little will be made ruler over much (Matt. 25:23, ESV). Many times, our trials and obstacles are really tests to see our faithfulness in action. Will we keep doing the right thing when the wrong thing is happening? Will we compromise our standards and ethics? Will we continue to love and develop the people we have, while waiting for the next influx of talent into our organization? Will we manage our money appropriately when we have a little so that we're prepared when we have an abundance? When we believe our trials are a test, we go to work to pass that test. When our trials appear to be pointless suffering, instead of rising to the occasion, we shrink back into misery. The fact is, nobody likes going through the test. But the test is the gatekeeper to the next level. Imagine it as sort of a final exam at this level of life. You can't go to senior year until you pass your junior year final. We want to be financially blessed, but we aren't passing the test with the little money we have. We want a bigger team, but we aren't loving and developing the team we have. We want to start the business, but we can't show up on time for the job we have. We want peace in our home, but we refuse to handle our own anger. Many of the setbacks

> **IN LIFE, IT'S LESSON REPEATED UNTIL LESSON IS LEARNED.**

and obstacles are really just holding periods. When we find ourselves stuck in life, many times, it's just a test to see how we will handle greater influence, responsibility, wealth, and power. Pass the test so you can level up.

2. TRIAL

When we are tried, our strength, resolve, and character are examined under real-life circumstances. During a trial, the evidence comes out. Trials produce the strength we need to bear the weight of leadership and influence. If tests examine our character, trials develop it. If you are going through a trying season, understand this; your strength, resolve, resourcefulness, mental toughness, and commitment are being forged and fortified so you will be prepared to enter a season of quantum growth. Ultimately, the trial makes us strong enough to enter into the next season of growth.

3. REFINING

Sometimes, the things holding us back from reaching our potential and moving from one level to the next are not things we lack, but rather, things that remain. Many times, it's not something new we need to learn; it's something old we need to let go of. Refinement is a process whereby we are required to remove the weights that we carry with us. It's about cutting off the things in our lives that stop us from being all that we could be. Imagine success as a trek up a rocky and treacherous terrain. Ahead of you is a magnificent mountain peak. At one of the checkpoints, you mistakenly forget your knapsack filled with 80 pounds of nonessential climbing gear. As you begin back up the mountain, you notice how much easier the climb is than it was before. In the same way, many of us are trying to traverse to another level in life carrying baggage that wasn't meant to make it up the mountain. The refining fire of the obstacle doesn't just equip us but it lightens us. When we understand the outcome and the purpose of the pain, it becomes possible to see all things from a perspective of gratitude. Even though, at the time, they may seem unpleasant, all things are part of the plan and process in our lives to become all we were meant to become.

When we operate in gratitude, the byproduct is experiencing a life of joy. Do you feel this world is cruel, unfair, or maybe that you haven't had a fair shake at life? While it is true we all have different experiences and circumstances that color our existence, life itself is both beautiful and cruel. There are competing truths and realities surrounding us at all points. For example, at any given time, there's both starvation in the world and incredible food to eat. There are both new births and an end to existing lives. The happiest people don't necessarily have the best of things, however, they *make* the best of things. At some point, we've got to decide what we're going to focus on and amplify in our life because what we think about, we bring about. We begin to attract to us the things that consume our minds. We are constantly moving toward our most dominant thought. If we can create a grateful and gracious mindset and a belief system that says all things are working for good, we attract more things to be thankful for and more peace, joy, and fulfillment as well.

MIRACLES IN THE MONOTONY

When you believe that life is special and you are here on purpose and for a purpose, you can begin to see the magic in the monotony. It's a belief system that creates peace, joy, happiness, and fulfillment, all of the things money, striving, likes, and sex can't provide.

I've chosen to accomplish this by raising my awareness of the miracles that exist in the mundane. We are surrounded by a multitude of miracles that have been lost in the monotony. If you have a car, you are in the top 1% of the world. If you have $1000, you are in the top 0.5% of the world. Every person you meet is a miracle. We can explain the process of reproduction and development, but we can't recreate it. Your neighborhood is a miracle. The fact that thousands of strangers, with their own self-interest, can peaceably and cooperatively live for the betterment of the whole is incredible. The modern medicine that gives us longer and more fulfilling qualities of life is a miracle. The flowers on the trees, which construct themselves from the nutrients in the ground and the rays from the sun, are miracles. Do you see the miracles all around you? Or are you blinded by the monotony of life? An attitude of gratitude allows you to see this incredible perspective. It's that perspective that truly makes life awesome. It's what gives you the power to love life, whether you are on top of the world or at rock bottom. Gratitude changes literally everything because it changes the way we view and relate to everything. We are wired by the Creator to have a deep vein of gratitude running through us. After all, as personal finance personality, radio show host, author, and businessman Dave Ramsey says, [We are all] "better than [we] deserve[13]." We are, at the most basic level, byproducts of our beliefs.

CHAPTER 5

ACTION

ac·tion

/ˈakSH(ə)n/

noun

1. the fact or process of doing something, typically to achieve an aim.

2. a thing done; an act.

"she frequently questioned his actions"

———

When everything has been said and done,
usually a lot more has been said than done.

In a world full of talkers, be a doer. It's what separates you from the masses. While most are bent toward preparing, analyzing, and learning, you must be bent toward doing. Don't just do it, do it big! Imagine a large jumbo jet, sitting on the runway, getting ready to take off. That plane, in order for it to soar into the sky, has to reach a terminal speed. Terminal speed is the level of speed required to get the lift needed for take-off. It's not enough for it to just move, it has to be moving fast. Likewise, you can't just move, you have to be moving fast. It's like the old adage says, you can be on the right track, but you will get run over if you are standing still. Success loves speed. Even if the plane is facing the complete opposite direction of its

IN A WORLD FULL OF TALKERS, BE A DOER.

intended target during takeoff, once it's airborne, it can quickly right its course and be back on track in no time. The same is true with leaders who take massive action. Even if they are headed in the wrong direction, the sheer force and speed of the action allow them to figure this out quickly and make the necessary course corrections while others are still planning. Here's the truth: no matter how good your plan is, the cleanliness of theory is no match for the messiness of reality. Some things you can't learn until you get up in the air, you can't plan for them, anticipate them, or create a model for them. You only learn through experiencing them. Those who take action learn information more fully and much faster than those who just ponder and pontificate. Action gives us feedback we can use to correct our course, refine our process, and move closer to the results we desire. Action, in a way, is a self-fulfilling prophecy. It's through action that we get the data necessary to make more efficient actions. The goodies in life will always go to those who do.

Everyone wants to wait for everything to be just right before they act. But the environment will never be just right. We need to learn to move first and question second. All the answers in the world aren't useful if we aren't applying them through action. Ready, fire, aim! Take the shot and course correct along the way. You'll end up infinitely better off than those still aiming.

Just move! No matter how you feel, move, or act, do something right now to move you in the direction of your stated goals and dreams. Many great accomplishments have been achieved quite by accident. Many times, the achiever sets out on a path towards one goal but, along the way, gets redirected by providence, changing market conditions, or stumbling across a byproduct much more revolutionary

WE NEED TO LEARN TO MOVE FIRST AND QUESTION SECOND.

than the intended product ever was. When you are moving, you have momentum, and momentum can easily be redirected from a place of action. This is especially true in the fabled story of Christopher Columbus who failed to reach the East Indies and ended up in the Americas. The fact is, he didn't exactly know what he was going to experience but he acted anyway.

SCRUM

Think about the smartphone you're holding in your hands right now. As I write this book, the iPhone 14 is in pre-launch, promising an array of new gadgets and technologies that the previous versions didn't have. One of the best ways to understand the bend towards action is to understand how the scrum model is applied in technology. The scrum method requires we bring our ideas to market rapidly and incompletely and let the market direct improvement. Apple didn't wait until it had all of the technology for the iPhone 12 to release an iPhone. It released iPhone 1, received feedback from its consumers on what was important to them, and made the changes for iPhone 2. The iPhone 3 and 4 were developed in the same manner. Today, 15 years later, the iPhone is a constant work in progress, and yet, it has created a mass market share with its imperfections along the way. We are the iPhone. We are not now the best that we will ever be, but we've got to take action to market, with all its inconsistencies, and allow the market forces to shape and mold our future self. We cannot wait until we deem our product perfect before taking action.

YOU CAN'T BALANCE A BICYCLE STANDING STILL

Have you ever tried to just sit on a stationary bike? It's quite literally impossible. Because you have no forward momentum, it is impossible to maintain balance on an upright bicycle for more than a few seconds. Yet, when that same bicycle has forward momentum or even backward momentum, you can maintain balance virtually indefinitely. The bicycle is a metaphor for our life. Without forward momentum, we're out of balance. We are meant to keep moving.

The motion creates the ability to balance and gives you a forward momentum, even through failure. While most people are analyzing and overthinking, the leader is taking massive action toward their dreams. It's been said that a poor decision on Monday is better than a good one on Friday. Why? Because by Wednesday, you realize the decision was poor, and you are on to the correct decision Thursday, a day ahead of time.

WE ARE MEANT TO KEEP MOVING.

Amateurs fear action for the possibility that the action could be wrong. But remember this, inaction is always the most costly action. Outstanding leaders understand that there really is no permanent wrong action. There are right actions and actions you learn from. Here's the key: action is the mother of all learning. It teaches you lessons much more quickly and vibrantly than learning alone would ever do. It condenses the timeframes and stakes between lessons and allows you to learn, progress, and change rapidly. I want you to remember your driver's training. As much as you could read and reread the book and take test after test, at the end of the day, there is simply no substitute for physically driving the vehicle.

INACTION IS ALWAYS THE MOST COSTLY ACTION.

No amount of book smarts about driving will ever replace the lessons learned by actually driving. At some point, we need to stop thinking and start *doing* because when we know by doing, there is no gap between what we know and what we do.

Everything good in life comes from action. At some point, all of our good intentions and great ideas have to move from intentions and ideas to execution. Execution is action. We need to act on what we know. Researching gyms online isn't going to help you lose weight. In fact, going to the worst gym in the world will help you lose more weight than researching the best gym in the world online. Action is what separates the greats from the average and ordinary. There are many great ideas, but very few execute them. All outstanding leaders have a bent toward action. They get things done, take chances, experiment, and take new ground. While everyone else is discussing the possible solution, the leader is out finding one. All great things in life are commissions. Commissions are made possible only through actions. Everything, from the house you live in, to the car you drive, to your spouse, and your bank account are commissions paid on actions taken. Think of the helpless romantic who loves the girl but never tells her. He doesn't get the girl, but someone who acts does.

You will never know all you would like to know. At some point, you must act on the information you have. Leaders learn to trust their gut, making the best choice possible with the available information.

THE DEATH OF CERTAINTY

Most people won't act until they are certain. The problem is, nothing in life is certain, except death and taxes. Most people seem to want to know just a little more, see the path just a little clearer, and wait for a moment just a little better, but here's a secret: nothing is certain. No matter how much we know or how much information we try to obtain, we will always have an incomplete picture. It's our ability to take action in spite of a lack of total clarity that sets us apart and helps us win big.

THE ACTION THRESHOLD

Newton's law: "An object at rest remains at rest, and an object in motion remains in motion . . . unless acted on by an unbalanced force."[14] The action threshold is best described as the relative amount of certainty someone must have or feel before taking action. Different people, with different personality types, have different action thresholds, meaning, the same decision to act will require more certainty in some people and less in others. Imagine two people looking at the same investment opportunity. One person may need to get to a certainty level of six before making an investment, while the other needs a certainty level of eight before making the same investment. The lower our action threshold, the more action we take.

Great leaders are always working to lower their action threshold. Knowing this about yourself and others is crucial. As discussed in my previous book *Byproduct*, there are four sorts of dominant personality traits with dozens of less dominant characteristics that color them. According to the DiSC Profile[15], the personality types are as follows: DOMINANCE personalities, INFLUENCE-based personalities, STEADINESS personalities, and CONSCIENTIOUSNESS personalities. Ranked in this order, they tend to have lower action thresholds with the Dominance personality type and get higher with every following trait, leaving the Conscientiousness personality trait as the highest action threshold. While this is good information to possess, it is in every leader's best interest to develop and lower their action threshold to the lowest levels possible. Leaders comprehend that very few actions can't be undone by better and larger actions. Many opportunities are missed because of indecision or procrastination.

THE ACTION QUOTIENT

| AMPLITUDE | X | PRECISION | X | TIME | = | RESULT |

ACTION QUOTIENT

When it comes to action, there are actually three components of the action that make it profitable. The action quotient reads as follows: amplitude x precision x time = results.

All of our outcomes, all of our results, in every area of life, are filtering through this equation. The good, bad, and ugly are all the products of amplitude x precision x time. Let's explore this formula.

Many times, we're doing the right things, we're just not doing them enough. This is called a critical mass of action. Critical mass is the idea that something needs to be of a certain size before it functions properly. Think about a giant metal dam holding back the waters of a rushing river. You can have the design, and the right material, but if it isn't big enough, it's not going to work. Water will rush around the sides and over it. It's the same concept with critical velocity. A plane requires a ground speed of at least X to lift off the ground, defy gravity, and fly. The same airplane, with the same equipment, but going X-1 will never take off. This is how amplitude works within the action quotient. How much action is being taken and at what rate? The action you are taking may be the correct action, but your amplitude, the size, or the amount of it you're taking may not be enough to hit that critical mass. When it comes to action when in doubt, double the amount. Most people are quick to doubt themselves, their skill set, and the eventual outcome of the project, but are slow, if ever, to look at the amount of action they are taking. More times than not, the thing that needs to change is the amount of action. Only once the critical mass of action has been reached is success possible. Going to the gym will help you lose weight and become more fit. This is true, sort of. Going to the gym once isn't going to help much. Going to the gym 4 times a week for 2 years is. It's the same action but with critical mass applied. It's not just the right action, but the right action, in large enough amounts, determines your level of success.

PRECISION

Precision is the accuracy with which an action is taken. Not all action is created equal. Imagine firing a pistol at a target one hundred times. Provided your accuracy (PRECISION) is adequate, that's enough action to eliminate the target. Theoretically, if you had a very precise shot, it would only require one shot to take the target down. Yet, while only one may be required, it might be noted that even after one hundred shots, if the PRECISION of the shooter is low, the target still may not have been hit. It's the right action (shooting), it's the right amplitude (more than enough)

NOT ALL ACTION IS CREATED EQUAL.

but that right action in the right amount is being carried out with low precision. Precision is another way to view and understand the role of skill. Skills pay the bills. High action and low skill equal worn out. Low action and high skills equals efficiency but broke. High action and high skill equals massive success. Have you ever been to the gym and witnessed a well-intentioned but lowly skilled athlete doing a workout with completely horrendous form? You watch in dismay as they hurl their body about like Gumby trying to lift weights that are far too heavy. They're putting out a lot of effort but getting little to no return for that effort. Instead of isolating the resistance on the muscle group being targeted, it divides the resistance into lots of secondary muscle groups assisting with the sporadic motions. Many would-be leaders look similarly ridiculous as they do and do and do, with underdeveloped skill sets. Given that the other variables of amplitude and time stay the same, growing our skill set guarantees that we grow our results because the same action is applied to a more successful and targeted filter.

TIME

My mentor Art Williams, a multi billionaire, used to say, "Almost everybody can stay excited for 2 or 3 weeks, a few people will stay excited for 2-3 months, but a winner will stay excited for however long it takes to get the job done."[16] The time is going to pass anyway. The question is, what will you have to show for it at the end? Why not pass the time moving in the direction of your dream? Here's what I've learned: Quitting won't speed it up. Even though your dream may feel like it's taking too long, remember that being late is better than never. Most people attempting to improve their life struggle with giving action and PRECISION enough time to allow the compounding of efforts. It's said that most people overestimate what they can do in a year and underestimate what they can do in a decade. Great things take time, and it's important to learn the patience principle when we decide to do something great.

QUITTING WON'T SPEED IT UP.

THE PATIENCE PRINCIPLE

Great things don't come to those who wait, leftovers do. Patience is a virtue, as long as it's the right kind of patience. The patience principle says: We must, as leaders, learn to be patiently impatient, patient with the process and impatient with ourselves. We must learn to be patient with the things we can't control—others, the process, the economy—and impatient with the things we can—our attitude, our effort, and our activity. When we are patient with the process but impatient with ourselves, we are driven to act and to change what we can, while not getting stressed and frustrated by trying to control the things we can't. This is the opposite of what most people do. They are frustrated about all of the things they can't control and yet do not attempt to control *themselves*. Patience is a virtue, only when we are patient with the right things.

GREAT THINGS DON'T COME TO THOSE WHO WAIT, LEFTOVERS DO.

MOMENTUM

A giant ten-ton freight train violently blows its horn as it lets everyone in the yard know it's leaving the loading dock. The engineer slams it into gear, and the beast roars, as it revs up to take off. Yet, there's no movement at all. The engineer, puzzled, hits the accelerator again. This time, the engine shrieks harder but still no movement. Now bewildered, the engineer jumps out of the engine to the tracks and begins to inspect the engine car. Everything looks fine; there's nothing jammed or stopped, and he thinks to himself, *there's nothing wrong with this train.* He bends to take one last look underneath the front of the train, and to his surprise, he sees two 2-inch blocks of wood propped between the front wheels of the train and the tracks. The blocks had been used to keep the train in place while it wasn't being used.

That same train can take over half a mile to stop; that same train can bulldoze through a concrete wall with no problem when it's moving. But, it can't budge even an inch when being stopped by a two-inch piece of wood. And there you have momentum. It's the same train; with momentum, you can't stop it, even if you try, and without it, a 2-inch block can keep it from ever getting started. Momentum takes bad players and makes them look good and good players and makes them look great. Momentum takes average teams and puts them in the Super Bowl. Much of life is about creating enough momentum to leap from one level to the next. This is why more people don't radically improve their situation. Like the locomotive, they give life the gas, but their thoughts, beliefs, and actions are acting as a 2-inch stopper. When you don't have momentum, even 2-inch blocks can seem like mountains.

Momentum is the byproduct of consistent action. Think about momentum this way. Imagine 5 kids in a swimming pool. If they are all doing their own things, everyone is using their own energy for their own actions. But, if the kids get in sync and begin to walk around the perimeter of the pool in the same direction, they can begin to create momentum. The same action is now easier than before, with each member benefiting from the actions and efforts of the other members. After some time, movement with momentum becomes almost effortless, and the whirlpool effect sweeps everyone in the pool away. That's how great teams, great businesses, and great leaders do it. They create a current of momentum in their organization. What was once difficult becomes easier and easier, and our facilities can then be directed towards building even greater momentum.

MOMENTUM KILLERS

Consider the game of basketball. For the most part, teams answer each other, point for point. On one side of the court, a team scores. Then, the other team runs the ball back and they score, and the drill goes on until one of the teams sparks the fire of momentum and goes on a run. All of a sudden, it's 10 or 12 unanswered points and a gap in the score of the game emerges. The energy in the stadium is electric as the crowd instinctively tunes into the display of raw momentum. It's at this point, every great coach calls a timeout. Their goal: to interrupt the train of momentum. Virtually always, the timeout will kill the momentum and reset the two sides into a point-to-point platform. The coach's use of timeout is strategic. He needs to stop the rush of momentum against his team.

While his use of the timeout is strategic, sadly, many people are calling a timeout on themselves, unwittingly disrupting the momentum starting to build. Poorly placed time off, little getaways, the "just

BUILDING MOMENTUM IS A 7-DAY-A-WEEK COMMITMENT.

this time" cheat meal, the weekend, these are all examples of the timeouts we call on ourselves. While all these things are necessary, most people seem to have a very low awareness of the role of momentum in their lives and tend to reward themselves with these timeouts at the worst possible times.

The reason most people are "most people" is they don't understand or respect the power of momentum in their lives. Building momentum is a 7-day-a-week commitment. Once the whirlpool in the water is turning strong, you can afford interruptions. If you interrupt it before momentum is solidly established, when you return, there won't be any momentum. Am I advocating you work 7 days a week and never take a break? Absolutely not. I am, however, challenging the concept of the traditional approach to working 8 hours for 5 days forever. A better concept than the middle-of-the-road approach is a front-loaded approach. Lots of constant, continual, uninterrupted effort in the beginning until momentum is established. Then, strategic, time away, while maintaining and growing momentum, until the current of success is so strong, you can step away for longer and longer periods of time.

This is exactly the strategy I used to create a semi-state of retirement for myself by the age of 32. I front-loaded effort for 7 days a week for the first 18 months in business. The next 18 months were 6 days a week. 3 years in, I was able to begin leaving the business for extended periods of time. Within 5 years, I was able to completely detach for 3-4 months at a time and the momentum of the organization would keep it moving. Are you unwittingly calling a timeout on yourself?

DISTRACTIONS

Distraction equals destruction when it comes to building momentum. Momentum is unidirectional. Like in the example of the pool, if everyone is moving in different directions, the momentum never builds as the actions counter the other actions. Only consistent effort applied in the same direction creates momentum.

Distractions are actions in other directions. One of my favorite maxims is this: you can have just about anything you want, but you can't have everything you want, at least not at the same time. How many people do you know with great ambition and energy, but they divert that energy in lots of different directions? They are volunteering here, in this workout regimen there, starting this business here, and traveling there. And it all looks like fun, but the law of momentum eventually will limit that person's effectiveness because their focus is diverted.

DISTRACTION EQUALS DESTRUCTION

Momentum creation requires 100% focus for a period of time. Am I saying that to create momentum you can only do one thing? Absolutely not. What I am saying, however, is if you want to create momentum, you can probably only do one thing at a time. If you are on a budget and you decide you want to start eating organic, great, but if you also want to get out of debt, the focus of your money dissipates. You may have to pick one to focus on and build momentum behind. Once the momentum is there, you can divert some of the focus onto the next priority. Distractions are anything that diverts focus energy or resources from the most important task.

Distractions can be especially aggressive momentum killers because they don't always appear as negative things. Some distractions, we can easily identify as negative and avoid. Others appear in the form of opportunity, fun, relationships, and relaxation. There's nothing wrong with these other than that they divert resources and focus from the main thing. To create momentum, we must be willing to give up what we want now for what we want most. When we have what we want most, we can go back and color our lives with all the pleasantries we passed along the way.

MOMENTUM TAKERS

In any organization, business, church, class, or peer group, there are two sorts of people. Momentum makers and momentum takers. Momentum makers are the ones that set the direction and tone. They create a culture and defend it. They do the heavy lifting of organizational direction. Momentum takers are people along for the ride. They aren't actively contributing to momentum, they are simply enjoying the fruits of it. Think about the pool again. If you have five kids creating the current and one just riding in it, the rider will create drag against the forming current but likely not enough to stop it. However, if you had only three creating the momentum and three just swirling in the current, the momentum will be much harder to create and dissipate much more quickly. If only one was creating the current and the other five were riding it, the momentum would never start.

Are you a momentum creator or a momentum taker? In every organization, we need to have processes in place to identify these momentum killers. If they can't be redirected to create momentum, they must be moved out of the organization. Momentum takers create drag on great organizations. Eventually, all organizations enter stagnation and decline. This happens when the ratio of momentum and culture creators is overrun by those simply benefiting from but not contributing to it.

Three things are required to create a movement of momentum. At any given point, we either have momentum or wish we did. Every great leader is fighting to create or maintain a tailwind of momentum in their organization. They understand that organizational effort is multiplied or divided by the presence or lack of real, tangible momentum. When their teams, churches, and organizations have momentum, anything is possible. As their belief expands, the action expands, and the cycle of momentum is unleashed. When there is no momentum, the organization's belief screeches to a halt, morale goes down, and work slows. As a leader, one of your primary jobs is to cultivate and sustain these game-changing bursts of momentum. Any momentum will require these three parts.

1. A PIONEER

The pioneer is someone who sees the momentum before it happens. They have vision. They fight back against the status quo before anyone else. The pioneer's effort starts the momentum cycle. It is often the work that carries the heaviest weight with the least return. Pioneers see the vision, share the vision, and live the vision. Many times, they are the lone voice in the wilderness, calling out for a better future.

In the fall, you can see large flocks of Canadian geese heading South for the winter. They fly in beautifully shaped V formations which scientists have studied extensively. Flying, sometimes thousands of miles with very little rest, these birds seem to have the efficiency of momentum down to a science. Scientists have found that the leader of the flock works up to 30% harder than birds at the back of the flock who are benefiting from the momentum and dispersion of the drag caused by the air. In other words, it's heavy lifting and hard work to be at the front of the pack. Because of this, the geese take turns, rotating out the front bird in the pack to give those creating the momentum an opportunity to benefit from the reduced effort of the momentum.

2. EARLY ADOPTERS

Momentum is all about movement. Early adopters are the people who most quickly identify and latch onto the new direction set by the pioneer. The early adopter helps to carry the load and champion the cause of the pioneer. The early adopters often face criticism for their belief in the new direction, but together, they walk. As more and more early adopters join the cause, the energy begins to build, and for the first time, the new direction can be seen and felt by outsiders. Early adopters bring two things to the cause. Number one is social proof. Social proof is the appearance of viability through social acceptance. Think about the good restaurant effect. You might drive by a restaurant with a line stretching around the block. You've never been there. You don't know anything about it, but it's likely to assume that it must be good because there are so many people waiting for the experience. The early adopter provides social proof and validation, both for the visionary and their movement. The second thing the early adopter provides is relief for the visionary. Like the Canadian geese swapping out birds at the head of the V, the early adopter can help lift some of the load required to create the necessary momentum.

3. THE MASSES TO ENGAGE

For full-blown momentum to occur, it must leave the realm of the few. When the masses adopt an idea, a feeling, or a belief, large numbers of people's effort, energy, and emotion are exerted and everyone notices. Where are you in the three stages of developing momentum? If you are a visionary, identify your early adopters. If you are an early adopter, who is someone else you can engage to adopt?

Think about the basketball analogy again. It's tight, neck and neck, and suddenly, the superstar makes a game-changing play. They shift the direction of the game. The other players on the team, inspired by the action, begin to believe and play with more confidence, adding to the momentum. Two points, then four, then six. At this point, the crowd in the stadium and the viewers at home adopt the momentum of the run, and everyone in the building is invested at some level.

What's going to happen next? How many more can we score before the timeout? What's the next play going to hold? Players and fans alike are electrified waiting on every move. That's the momentum process: started by a visionary, a leader, or a game-changer, adopted by the early adopters, and officially pushed to momentum by the crowd. Decide today you are going to be a momentum maker and not a momentum taker. Understand the three factors needed to create momentum and start letting momentum carry you further than you ever could have dreamed.

CHAPTER 6

SYSTEMS: DON'T JUST DO, AUTOMATE

sys·tems
/ˈsistəm/

noun

1. a set of things working together as parts of a mechanism or an interconnecting network.

2. a set of principles or procedures according to which something is done; an organized framework or method.

I s what you are doing right now getting you out of doing what you're doing right now? One of my mentors asked me that question early in my career. I was great at doing but less great at teaching and replicating. He challenged me to look beyond performing and into replication, duplication, and scale.

A personality-driven business isn't worth much six feet underground. Great leaders, whether in the home, at church, or in a business, without great systems, EVENTUALLY CEASE to be great leaders. They get burnt out, overwhelmed, and become unproductive. Systems are, in essence, the value of the entity. Sooner or later, 100% of the human capital running it will no longer be around. There are exactly zero people working for Ford Motor Company today that were there in the beginning, yet Ford persists. The

IS WHAT YOU ARE DOING RIGHT NOW GETTING YOU OUT OF DOING WHAT YOU'RE DOING RIGHT NOW?

truly iconic businesses, the companies that last for generations, survive solely on their culture and systems. The systems of the business allow for duplication and scalability. The million or even billion-dollar question is this: What are you doing manually, today, that could be done by a system?

Systems and automation aren't bad, and they aren't competing for jobs. They free us from mundane and monotonous tasks, allowing our minds to do what they do best, create, innovate, and act. They are taking care of the rudimentary and predictable processes. Systems bring value to the entity and leverage our time.

A PERSONALITY-DRIVEN BUSINESS ISN'T WORTH MUCH SIX FEET UNDERGROUND.

While people and leaders vary greatly in their views, ideas, and practices, systems create uniformity. Discretion is the enemy of duplication. Automation is the way we leverage our best ideas and processes, taking the best from our human capital and sharing it structurally through our organization. When a great coach is gone, their direct influence on and value to the team diminishes, eventually becoming zero, unless their thinking, methods, and processes were systematized. Then, even after they're physically gone, their ideas, processes, and procedures still exert influence. Systems allow us to produce and duplicate scalable results. Systems alone don't win for you, neither do great leaders. The greatest organizations have great systems driven by great leaders. When we automate as much of our process and responsibility as possible, we free up time, effort, and energy to be redirected into finding efficiencies, opportunities, and new ideas. Systems create predictable results that allow us to stay busy leading instead of producing.

Human capital is easily the most expensive part of operating any organization. The cost of acquiring, training, and keeping great people is immense. Even more costly is when you fail to retain great people. When key people leave, without systems, the knowledge and wisdom they accumulated in their position leave with them. When every layer of the organization is systematized, our organizations lose less to personnel loss. The person might be gone, but the knowledge and the process are left behind and intact. This leaves more time and attention to making forward motions instead

DISCRETION IS THE ENEMY OF DUPLICATION.

of recovering what was lost.

Early in my first business, virtually all of the training was done one by one and was dependent completely on me. Our presentations were incredibly effective and had a mid-90% close rate. The problem was, they were too good. They were spectacularly effective, but they were hard for new people to learn. There was a lot of information to assimilate. Only I and a few other agents were able to learn 14 pages of presentations ripe with tie-downs and referral hits. What I learned was I had to simplify to multiply. If something is 80% as effective, but can be learned twice as fast or by twice as many people, that's a win. Scale first, efficiency second.

When it comes to creating systems in your business, ministry, or life, there are 3 golden rules to remember:

1. REMOVE

What are you doing today that should no longer be done? What are we doing because it's the way we've always done it, because it's tradition, or because it's what our predecessors did? What are we doing that no longer moves the bottom line? That's break-even at best for our business that isn't exciting or electrifying or energizing? From individuals to ministries to multibillion-dollar corporations, all of us are doing things in our life that just don't matter. We've got to cut out the clutter. We've got to silence the noise and get to the heart of the matter. Every minute, dollar, and emotional measure of energy that we save by removing something that's no longer needed can be reinvested into systematizing the areas that are the game changers. This is super unpopular in action because everybody loves to hold on to the familiar. Many times, it's not about what you're doing, it's about what you *stop* doing that gives you the weightlessness you need to break the inertia and get into orbit. Many entities create elaborate systems and structures around things that shouldn't be there in the first place. Don't institutionalize the existence of bad ideas, bad products, and bad thinking.

WHAT ARE YOU DOING TODAY THAT SHOULD NO LONGER BE DONE?

2. SIMPLIFY—LOSING TO WIN

The longer and more complex something is, the more time and effort it takes to transfer it to someone else. Your entity will grow at the speed that your people can easily uptake and execute its systems and processes. When we decided to get serious about becoming a systems-driven business, the first thing we did was consolidate and clarify. We took the most important information, concepts, and processes from our presentations and reduced them from 14 pages down to 1. That's 14 times less information to transfer, learn, and memorize. The presentation time was reduced from 45 minutes to less than 12. Losing so much material, one would expect some reduction in quality. And that's what we experienced. The close ratio dropped from the low 90s to right at 80%. The new presentation was indeed less effective. But, it was easy to learn and quick to adopt. So, even though it was individually less effective, we were able to quickly scale from a few salespeople who were competent, to hundreds and then thousands who could quickly and easily learn and present the information. Even though individual results were slightly lower, the net result was an increase of hundreds of times the previous amount of production. Simplifying is the key to multiplying in every area possible.

3. UNIFORMITY

As I stated earlier, discretion is the enemy of duplication. Individual performance is a limit. It's like that old proverb: "If you want to go fast, go alone; but if you want to go far, go together" (Origin Unknown). Systemization is about taking the variables of human failure and human limitation out of the equation. A great system is something that can be run with little training and implemented quickly to acquire consistent and predictable results. Systems need to be streamlined, simple, and consistent. When everybody's doing their own thing, while the individual may be more productive, the whole actually slows down. Why? Because every piece in the process is dependent upon an individual's performance. What happens one day when that individual changes company or retires? When the knowledge that our entity holds is solely within the heads of the people, the organization's value ends with its tenure. One of the toughest choices I had to make as a leader was to change from an individual competency model to a systems-driven "competent whole" model.

For example, again using my former financial agency, there were certain individual agents who would modify the systems in place, and from time to time, get exceptional results. The results can be many times greater than that of the average person using just the system. The problem becomes evident when they try to duplicate their success in others. Their shortcuts or augmentations are often based on experience that they alone possess or on personality traits that are unique to them as an individual. So, when they try to transfer their success to others, they do so ineffectively because their "system" requires these certain individualized traits in order to work. By simplifying to multiply the individual may sacrifice some level of autonomy and creativity but the result of a competent whole in virtually every case far exceeds the value of the competent individual. Please understand me here, I'm not vying for less competent individuals, what I'm saying is that our system should not be driven to the highest quality performers, but should be standardized for the lowest quality performers. There is one glaring exception and that is in the area of research and development. Freedom to experiment, disassemble and reassemble the system, and look for ways to assimilate new best practices into current systems is a must.

SYSTEMS IN THE ORGANIZATIONAL GROWTH STAGES

It's important to understand that before you can have systems, you've got to have something to systematize. Many aspiring organizational leaders have elaborate systems and incredible business plans but no business and no people to use them with. Depending on what stage of growth your organization is in, your utilization of systems and processes will look different. At every level, we should look to systematize everything possible.

1. STAGE 1: START-UP PHASE AND ENTREPRENEURIAL PASSION

Whether we're looking at a business, a church plant, or a non-profit, all entities start out with what I call an entrepreneurial passion. Whether a business, a church, or a team, a zealous, idealistic, and charismatic leader is behind it. All forward momentum at this launch level is driven by the passion and excitement of the leader. In this stage, the organization is experimenting with almost every area of its existence. Its culture, its values, its momentum, all of it is created largely by the persona of the leader. During this phase of the organization's growth, momentum and forward movement are everything. The organization needs to be lean and decision-making, limited to a few key individuals. The systems and processes in this phase of the organization's growth pattern center around alleviating the visionary leader and top management from the daily and rudimentary tasks of running the business. This may be as simple as hiring support staff or creating community groups at the church to move some of the responsibility of building individual relationships with others within the organization. They might be as simple as documenting sales processes, manufacturing processes, or service structures, so they can be easily communicated to new additions to the team. Systems and processes here are generally built out of necessity and are created only when the organization ceases to be able to move further without them. This is what I call reactionary systemization and is where most businesses, churches, and organizations exist. They build systems and processes only as a means of necessity from moving from one area to the next. Here's the key: Great organizations proactively search out opportunities to systematize, simplify, and multiply. They aren't satisfied with simply reacting to needs as they arise but move from reaction to anticipation. There is no success without succession, and ultimately, systems and processes are what will allow the leader's vision to be successfully passed along to the next generation of leaders.

STAGE 2: EXPONENTIAL GROWTH

This stage occurs when the organization hits critical mass. It's got several leaders leading well, and its concepts, culture, visions, and rudimentary systems are in place. At this level, there is a magical combination of visionary leadership driving simplified systems. Leadership without the systems creates limits. Systems without visionary leadership create stagnation. The exponential growth phase of any organization is marked by the perfect marriage between visionary leadership and purposefully planned systems.

The growth, at this phase, is almost supernatural. It's at this phase when growth outpaces the current systems that more robust systems and processes must be developed. In this phase, a majority of the organization's productivity is happening on many levels removed from the direct influence of the visionary leader. The systems and processes need to allow people of average capabilities to act, think, and decide like the leader would, without having to have all of the leader's experience and leadership intangibles. Great systems and processes should be extensions of the visionary leader's thinking, values, decision-making, and understanding.

Consider the phenomenon of "Painting with a Twist", where groups of women gather in storefronts around the country to drink wine and paint. At the center of the class, an experienced painter takes a completed work of art and breaks down its component pieces, teaching the participants, stroke by stroke, how to recreate the original work. It is unnecessary for the participants to have the understanding or skill to be able to create the original painting on their own. In fact, it's unnecessary for them to even see the original work. If they follow the steps presented by the instructor, they will create, in most cases, a finished piece of art that resembles closely the original artwork. The participants do not need to study art for years. They do not need to understand the mixing of colors or the different sorts of techniques being used; they simply need to follow the process.

This is a great example of what systems and processes do in an organization. They allow people with far less skill and experience to generally reproduce the leader's original vision. Without the system, the participants would be forced to try to recreate the original all on their own. Many wouldn't know where to begin or would get lost along the way. They would have trouble understanding, in many cases, which steps should come first. Although the participants are working towards the same goal with the same materials, some will inevitably struggle to succeed. This is also the case for organizations that don't make the jump into systemization. The exponential phase is all about developing systems or going bust. Systems must be in place to produce predictable results and free up human capital to lead, innovate, and inspire. Having a great leader who knows how to use their gut and pick the right executive candidates or the right piece of property is great until that person isn't here anymore. Now what? Even that gut-driven leader has a system and a process underlying that ability. If they name it, describe it, and document it, their effectiveness lives on, even after they have moved on from their roles.

In Ray Dalio's book *Principles*[17], he discusses, at great length, how he systematized virtually every decision his team needed to make. Complex investment decisions, all the way down to simple trading processes were streamlined and systematized to free his team to grow and innovate. His systems are largely credited with allowing him to become one of the greatest hedge fund managers in history.

PHASE 3: MATURE COMPANY PHASE

It's at this phase that the company's systems and processes are largely intact and operational. Virtually all of the day-to-day decision-making on everything, from marketing to customer service to human resources, is made through systemization and processes, far removed from the visionary leader. It's also at this point that most companies stagnate, as they begin to rely more and more on systems and less and less on leadership. It's also in this phase that companies get lured into complacency and become targets for new innovative and up-and-coming companies in their space.

WHAT GOT US TO THIS LEVEL WILL NOT GET US TO THE NEXT LEVEL.

In this phase, streamlining, reinventing, and reevaluating the systems is key. What got us to this level will not get us to the next level. Many companies at this level settle into what has worked in the past and give little thought to the future. A great picture of this is the failed acquisition of Netflix by Blockbuster. Blockbuster was absolutely dominating its space when Netflix brought to them the idea of creating a streaming platform. Unwilling to reevaluate its current systems, processes, and capabilities, Blockbuster foolishly declined, assuming that its current systems would meet the demands of a changing world. Obviously, today with Blockbuster long gone and Netflix one of the most successful streaming services in the world, it's a case in point that many times our size and strength become hindrances. A lack of resources makes us scrappy, and resources in abundance make us lazy. As we become more successful, we tend to rest on the way things have always been done.

A LACK OF RESOURCES MAKES US SCRAPPY

We depend heavily on the systems and processes that created our success. But what worked yesterday is not what will work tomorrow. Visionary leaders in the mature company phase are constantly looking for opportunities and are constantly reevaluating, reconfiguring, and reinventing their systems and processes.

The earlier we begin to think system-minded and create documented processes, the earlier we create something of real value. The business, the team, and the church are, at their most basic level, a series of systems. When these systems are strong, the entity can be transferred from one leader to the next, one generation to the next, or be sold but still perpetuated. During the writing of this book, I sold one of my companies in an eight-figure transaction. The transition was virtually seamless because of the systems and processes I developed. I was able to transfer the business with no interruption to the new owner. If the system is nonexistent, or not easily transferable, then you have nothing of real value. You don't own a business, you are self-employed. You don't have a church, you are a church. Whether at a company, a church, or a high school music program, a leader is tasked with taking their skills, knowledge, passion, and processes and teaching them to others. A system's success is found in the organization's ability to continue without you. A real leader is tasked with working themselves out of a job.

SYSTEMIZING HUMAN CAPITAL

Within every organization, whether a church, corporation, nonprofit, or little league team, there are three ways that people within the organization can be sorted. I call these engagement groupings. While there are hundreds of nuances that exist within the three groupings, it is imperative that every leader knows, understands, and can identify the people around them and their placement within these groups. The groupings are essential for leaders to understand where their time should be spent and which people provide the greatest opportunity for leverage and growth. It's also worth being noted that every personality type we discussed earlier in the book can exist within each of these engagement-level groups. The engagement-level groupings are helpful in understanding how different people engage and relate to the organization, not how the people are on an individual level.

1. PLAYERS

Players are people within the organization that are on the field. They aren't spectating; they are playing the game. They are models of culture, work ethic, drive, and other positive traits the organization stands for. They understand their roles and play them well. They also understand their roles extend beyond just their performance, and their example, leadership, and demeanor are actually shaping that of the organization at large. They are able to not only perform as individuals but they understand the impact their performance, attitude, words, and examples have on the team as well. Players are the people you love to have around; they are bought into the vision, they are flexible and adaptable, and generally operate with a whatever-it-takes mentality. They are the trifecta of hunger, skill, and character. These people are multipliers in the organization; they are leverage points. Time, money, and training invested in players yield huge returns for the organization.

An investment in a player isn't just being invested in that one person. Players turn around and deploy it back into the organization. Retired football coach Urban Meyer talks about these people as the inner circle. Their shadows in the organization extend far beyond themselves. They are directly, or indirectly, responsible for the movement or stagnation of the team. Recognizing who holds this spot on your bus is essential for all leaders. These people impact every level of an organization. As leaders, these are the people who will help us execute change and communicate initiatives. They are invaluable to an organization. This uncommon trifecta of hunger, skill, and character takes time, sometimes decades, to develop. Trying to take someone new to the organization and move them to the inner circle takes time, effort, and resources. It's imperative that leaders build strong relationships and a high speed of trust with their inner circle. Think of the inner circle as a gravitational pull that the rest of the organization orbits around. The stronger and more massive the inner circle, the stronger the pull and the more orbiters it can amass.

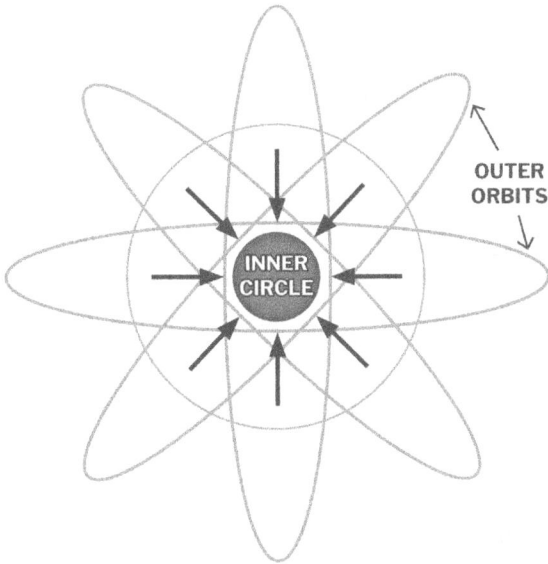

Organizations that scale have an inner circle of sufficient gravitational pull to sustain the growing demands of the objects in orbit around it. As a leader, if your inner circle doesn't exist, or you don't have a plan to keep and develop that inner circle, you will never achieve scale. You can't build the orbiting rings of the organization without a solid core.

Another uniqueness of the inner circle, the player, is their ability to see their impact on the organization as a whole. The inner circle is the only part of an organization that seeks to reproduce itself and grow. Every other subsection of the organization largely exists in a vacuum, only able to see its own interests.

A player understands that by developing and recruiting other players, the heavy lifting of the organization actually becomes easier.

Remember the friends in the pool attempting to create a current from earlier in the book? As they begin to move in a unified direction, it is cumbersome and slow-moving. But as the current begins to flow, each step becomes easier and easier, assisted by the force of the current being created. At this point, momentum sets in and the current's power moves everything in its way. The player is a current creator.

2. COULD-BE PLAYERS

Could-be players are people within the organization with the capacity to become successful players, but they lack the commitment or skill set needed to function as a player. They could have influence but are largely unaware of that influence or don't attempt to harness it. They are part of the group creating the current, sometimes. With enough time, effort, and investment, could-be players can be transformed into full-blown players. Here's the key though. While it looks like these are the people we should be spending the most time and effort developing, as leaders, we can't develop people. People develop *themselves*. We can only provide the resources and environment to help them develop. Our job, as a leader, is to give people an environment and an example. The rest is up to the person.

This is where so many leaders burn out. They spend massive amounts of time and resources investing in could-be players because they see their potential. They make one fatal flaw that costs organizations countless hours and resources. What is that fatal flaw? We erroneously believe that with enough time and attention, *WE* can transform these could-be players into players. *WE* can't transform anyone; we can only equip them to transform themselves. Time, effort, and resources directed to could-be players should, as much as possible, be done in group settings. Where a player might be afforded the opportunity of working with a performance

> **WE CAN'T TRANSFORM ANYONE; WE CAN ONLY EQUIP THEM TO TRANSFORM THEMSELVES.**

coach, that same coach might be used to facilitate a small group session with the could-be players. We need to give them the opportunity to develop while understanding they may never choose to use that opportunity.

3. VERY NICE PEOPLE

Very nice people are just that. They are very nice. They are grateful for the job, or the team, or whatever. They do their job … most of the time. But they are only going with the flow. They aren't directing the flow. These people want to do their job and be done. They are not operating with the same level of intensity, direction, or motivation as the player or could-be player. They are where they are, know what they know, do what they do, and get what they get. They aren't concerned much with changing that. Very nice people want to do their job and be left alone. They don't see the need for involvement in the culture. They generally aren't concerned with the progress of the organization or their personal progress. They are content where they are. Very nice people, generally, will make up somewhere between 40-80% of your organization, depending on the type of organization you are a part of.

What to do with very nice people: Let them know they are appreciated. Praise them when they do a good job. Correct them privately when they don't. Let them work at their own pace and in their own way. Don't try to force growth on them.

What not to do with very nice people: Don't ask them about their numbers, don't ask them to participate as a group, and don't force them into cooperative work, if not essential.

Many people reading this who run organizations may look at the three groups of people and ask: why even keep the very nice people as part of your organization? Why not just transition them from the entity? The answer is simple. No matter what sort of organization you run, how large or small, your talent will always eventually reside in one of these groups. Even in the NBA, with the highest performers from around the world, there will be superstars, starters, and benchwarmers. If you were to remove all of the people at the bottom, the remaining people would eventually group into players, could-be players, and very nice people again.

A 4TH-TIER OF PERSON, SUSPECTS

Suspects are people who, at some point, occupied one of the previous three levels but have since soured. You can see it in their eyes; you can sense it in their sophisticatedly cynical attitudes. They aren't just underperforming, they are actually working against the current of the organization and its leadership. These are people with a vendetta; passed up for a promotion, offended by a supervisor, or any number of reasons. In every team, a small percentage of people will be drilling holes in the boat while everyone else is rowing, and if they aren't yet, they will be.

THE LAST PART OF A PERSON THAT TRULY COMMITS TO AN ORGANIZATION IS THE HEART.

People get involved in an organization in this way: First, their body shows up. They are physically present, but they aren't all-in. They tend to be primarily motivated by their own wants and needs. The second thing that shows up is their mind. They mentally engage in the process, project, or performance. They aren't just physically there anymore, they are applying their mental capacities to moving the leader's vision. The last part of a person that truly commits to an organization is the HEART. When the heart shows up, they are no longer a part of something, that something belongs to them and they belong to it. They have unified with the vision. The organization's beliefs are their beliefs, the goals are their goals, and the defeats are their defeats. These people, the ones that play with heart, are the protectors and defenders of the culture. They are the ones that move the organization forward. This is important to understand because everyone in every organization is somewhere on the joining continuum. At all times, everyone can be found somewhere on the scale. Great leaders understand that one of their primary functions in developing human assets is to create a culture and environment that systematically creates opportunities to engage and move team members down the continuum.

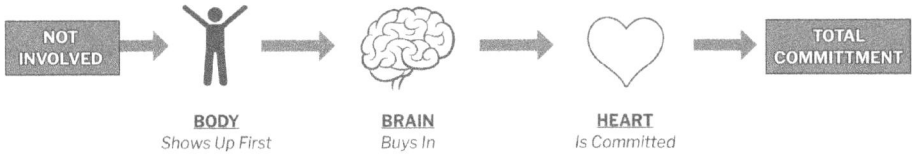

NOT INVOLVED				TOTAL COMMITMENT
BODY	BRAIN	HEART		
Shows Up First	Buys In	Is Committed		

It is also true that as people join an organization in three steps, they leave the entity by the same three-step process. Just in reverse. The first thing to leave when someone begins the process of exiting their organization is the heart. Something or someone severed the tie, and this teammate just doesn't connect the way they once did. The skies just aren't as blue, the roses just don't smell quite the same. They just don't have that same edge they possessed before. As leaders, it's important for us to recognize the amount of time, resources, and investment it takes in someone to move them from showing up, to showing up mentally, to showing up with heart. Our environments, policies, and procedures must be constantly scanned for disengagement points that sever the heart relationship with the organization.

It's important to understand very few people within an organization are aware of this process and how to recognize it. Leaders MUST be trained in the principles of personnel engagement. There's a study that recently came out that said somewhere above 70% of workers are disengaged or actively disengaged at their job.[18] That is a gigantic opportunity for growth improvement and acceleration. The leader that can succeed at actively engaging his or her people is one that will run circles around the competition every time.

After the heart disconnects, the next thing that goes is the mind. They mentally check out from the goal, the mission, and the process. They are just doing their time and collecting a check. They live an existence of going through the motions. They are physically there, but nobody's home. The goals of the team are no longer their goals, the heartbeat of the team is no longer their heartbeat. The whole person is no longer showing up, just a shell of what the person used to be. These people are no longer willing to go above and beyond. They aren't willing to lend their ideas to improvement; they show up, do the job, and then leave, every day dying a little more inside.

Eventually, the discontentment of showing up day after day, at one place, when your heart and mind are somewhere else, becomes too much to handle and finally, they physically leave, completing the exit process. Think about a job or a church or an organization you eventually left. Do you recognize these steps as having played out in your life? It starts by just not feeling it quite the same, the spark goes dim. You are still there, still serving, still contributing, but it just isn't the same. As time goes on, our attitude turns a bit soured. We ask ourselves, *Why am I giving so much here?* They don't … (fill in the blank) *about me.* We show up, but secretly, we long to leave, to be somewhere else, doing something else. The fire is out. We show up day after day out of a feeling of duty or respect, but we and everyone around us know it's just a matter of time.

While this is an extremely personal process, great leaders and teams can systematically influence how people join and stay in the organization. Here are some ways teams can influence the joining and leaving continuum.

1. RECOGNIZE IT

We must teach our people to see the process in action and be able to recognize the common characteristics and behaviors of people at different places on the continuum. We must help our people understand the importance of encouraging buy-in and staying bought-in; we must teach them how to recognize opportunities to help people buy-in and stay-in. Once we become more familiar with watching the joining and leaving processes in action, it becomes easier and easier to quickly and easily spot people in different parts of the process. When we know where in the process those people are, we can strive to create environments and opportunities to move them deeper into the continuum of commitment.

2. LOOK FOR HOLES IN THE FUNNEL

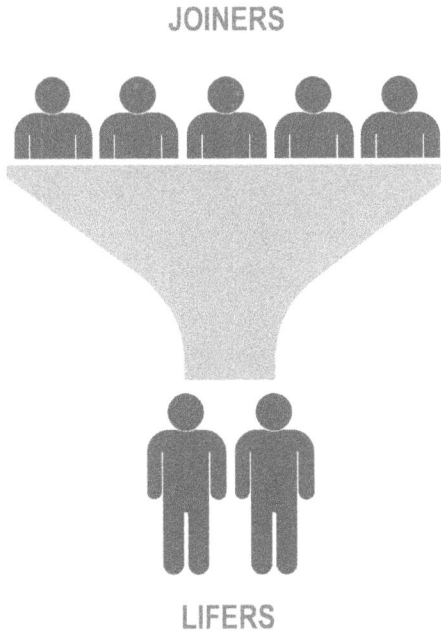

JOINERS

LIFERS

In any organization, there are holes in the funnel. There will always be more people at the top of the funnel than at the bottom. People at the top are joiners, and people at the bottom are lifers. In a perfect world, an ORGANIZATION would convert 100% of its joiners to lifers. Obviously unrealistic for a multitude of reasons, there are factors we can use to influence the number of people who do make it from the top of the funnel to the bottom. In your organization, there are funnel jams, areas in the process, where people seem to get stuck rather than progressing toward buy-in. By studying the way that people join, engage, and commit to things, we can identify and leverage these areas. They are our greatest opportunity for growth. This is an area I work extensively in with my executive, one-on-one-level consulting clients. Your ability to understand your system, and the common places people get caught in them, can save millions or 10s of millions of dollars and enormous amounts of time, effort, and emotional energy.

CHAPTER 7

ATTITUDE

at·ti·tude

/ˈadəˌt(y)o͞od/

noun

1. a settled way of thinking or feeling about someone or something, typically one that is reflected in a person's behavior.

———

Attitudes are contagious. Is yours worth catching?

In life, we can ultimately control two things: our attitude and our activity. Our attitude has more to do with our experience in life than almost anything else. Consider the saying: "The happiest people don't have the best of everything, they just make the best of everything they have."[19] Our attitude is completely within our control and always within our agency. We don't have to let the external state of affairs affect our internal state of being. It's not the water outside of the ship that makes it sink; it's the water that gets on the inside that makes it sink. We can endure

> **IN LIFE, WE CAN ULTIMATELY CONTROL TWO THINGS: OUR ATTITUDE AND OUR ACTIVITY.**

almost anything in life with the right mental attitude. An entire book could be dedicated to the subject of attitude. Here, we're going to focus on two of the most important attitudes that you can cultivate: enthusiasm and resistance to offense.

ENTHUSIASM

Nothing great has ever been accomplished without first having a great amount of enthusiasm.

Success is going from failure to failure, without a loss of enthusiasm. Your energy introduces you before you introduce yourself. Your state is contagious. Have you ever been around someone whose energy is just magnetic? They walk into the room and it lights up; everybody just loves being around them. That is state contagion. Their energy is affecting the energy of the people around them. Likewise, have you ever been around someone who is negative and lethargic and makes you feel worse about your life? It's the same phenomenon.

ENTHUSIASM IS NOT A FEELING; IT'S A DECISION.

I read somewhere, although I do not recall the source, Jimmy Johnson, head coach of the Dallas Cowboys between 1989 and 1994, said to his locker room of professional athletes every year, on the first day of training camp, that today we are going to have a ton of false enthusiasm! Because sooner or later, that false enthusiasm is going to turn into real enthusiasm. Enthusiasm, excitement, and passion are prerequisites to massive success. You simply won't put in the work necessary for big results, long enough, without them.

Enthusiasm allows us to take larger and more deliberate actions. Think about when you're really excited about something. How easy is it to get up in the morning? You almost can't wait. When you love something or you're passionate about something, you can do it all day and all night, day after day after day, and never need a break. In fact, the more you do it, the more you're energized. It's like a self-charging car battery, the faster the car runs, the more power the battery receives. Enthusiasm allows us to take big action. At this point, a lot of people tell me, "Well, what if I'm just not enthusiastic about what I'm doing, Ian?" Here's the key: Enthusiasm is an inside job. It's perspective. There are painters who can't wait for 5:00 o'clock to clock out and go back home, and there are painters who look at their skill as a work of art and work meticulously to get every line and every cut just right. It's the same job with a different perspective.

I want to challenge you to look for the meaning and purpose in what you're doing. You're serving somebody. You're helping somebody's life improve in some way. You may think what you're doing is not significant, but that's a lie. Without you, somebody, somewhere wouldn't have what they need. Learn to shift your perspective, and it's easy to come in every day and do your work with a spirit of excellence and enthusiasm. It also allows us to endure sustained action for longer periods of time. When we are excited about our destination, we are more likely to continue in that direction.

Enthusiasm is NOT a feeling; it's a decision. None of us are born with professional-level enthusiasm about something. Initially, there is interest, and over time, with effort and results, increasing levels of excitement and enthusiasm are cultivated. But even then, our level of enthusiasm and excitement is a choice. Some days, you're just not gonna feel like it. We have to choose, every day, to bring our "A" game when it comes to our attitude and our mental state.

It's not only what allows us to attract to us the necessary resources, support, and energy, but it's also what allows us to continue on past the point where most others stop and throw in the towel. Enthusiasm is the fuel for success.

WE CAN LEARN FROM ANYONE, AND WE SHOULD.

RESISTANCE TO OFFENSE

Welcome to the United States of Offense. Today, everyone is offended about everything. People wear their offenses as a badge of honor. Here's the truth: Offense is one of the greatest tools of the enemy. It closes you down when you should be open; it enrages you when you should be cool and collected.

If the enemy can get you offended by those you should be learning from, his work is done. There are people who are supposed to take you higher, but you have allowed offense to stop you from

WHAT YOU ALLOW TO OFFEND YOU SAYS MORE ABOUT YOU THAN THE PERSON DOING THE OFFENSE.

receiving from them. The fact is, we can learn from anyone, and we should.

Here's another truth, stop taking everything so personally. What you allow to offend you says more about you than the person doing the offense. Understand that most people are not thinking about you at all. Why allow someone or something not directed at you to steal your peace?

> **PEOPLE CAN TAKE MANY THINGS FROM YOU, BUT THEY CAN'T TAKE YOUR ATTITUDE AND EMOTIONAL STATE UNLESS YOU GIVE IT TO THEM.**

Don't lose your power. Control over one's state is the final frontier of control. People can take many things from you, but they can't take your attitude and emotional state unless *you* give it to them. When you give other people control of your emotions through offense, you give away *your* power.

OFFENSE PEDDLERS

People today usurp power through the medium of offense. When you are offended, you give your power away. That power is accumulated by the offense peddler. If you can get someone offended, you can get them off balance. When what someone else says or does controls your emotions, you are out of control. Don't give away your power, rather, decide to become UNOFFENDABLE.

You don't have to agree with someone to learn from them. In fact, wisdom says you learn the most from those you *disagree* with. People often use offense to dismiss having to learn from an interaction. They may think, *If I'm offended, that invalidates everything about this or I disagree with this person or I don't like this about them, so why should I look at any other area of their life?* The fact is, there are no perfect people. If you look to learn only from others who think and act exactly as you do, you won't learn much. Today, instead of being open, coachable, and willing to learn, most people think they already know. The chorus line of the broke and insignificant is "I know, I know" followed by the refrain of "I owe, I owe." Anything that doesn't align with what they already believe is offensive to them. The truth is, if it offends you, it's probably exactly what you need to be hearing.

Now, please, let me be clear, I'm not talking about offense at cultural stigmas, racism, and other things of that nature. I'm talking about personal offense, stemming from personal interaction. When you are offended by what the pastor says, when you are offended by what your mentor says, that's when the warning light needs to go off. That's probably an area of improvement for you. Climbing the mountain of success is hard enough on its own, let alone trying to scale the rocky walls with a 500-pound sack of offense on your back. The enemy will use offense more than anything else to block your blessing. When you are offended by the people God has put in your life to lead you, connect you, and bless you, you shut down the flow of his provision in your life. Here are a couple of tools you can use to become UNOFFENDABLE:

HONOR—HONOR ISN'T EARNED, IT'S GIVEN

Give people the benefit of the doubt and let them prove you wrong. Instead of becoming offended, try instead thinking, *Maybe there is a missing context to what this person said. Is there a perspective I'm missing?*

Believe it or not, most people have better things to do than piss you off. Certainly, from time to time, there are things that deserve righteous indignation, but for the most part, those are few and far between. When you waste all of your energy on offense, you won't have any left for

> GIVE PEOPLE THE BENEFIT OF THE DOUBT AND LET THEM PROVE YOU WRONG.

success. Everyone is valuable to God, and everyone has something valuable to teach you, even if it's what not to do. Don't be offended, be wise. Give the benefit of the doubt. Seek to understand and then to be understood. Most offenses could be solved by having an open and honest discussion about what happened. A lack of communication is almost always the source of offense. Start with honor.

RESPECT

Self-RESPECT

Respect for others is given. Self-respect is earned. It's probably the most important mental attitude we can cultivate. We know when we haven't paid the price, cut the corner, or haven't earned our stripes. And that lack of self-respect manifests in a thousand self-sabotaging iterations. Only after you respect yourself and not until, can you truly respect others. Respect for others is impossible without first respecting oneself. When we operate without self-respect, it is literally impossible to operate genuinely with respect for others, our environment, our surroundings, and life in general. When we don't treat ourselves with respect, is it any wonder when the world around us doesn't either? We teach the world and the people around us how to treat us, first and foremost, by our example of how we treat ourselves.

> **RESPECT FOR OTHERS IS GIVEN. SELF-RESPECT IS EARNED.**

RESPECTING OTHERS

Start from a place of respect for all and watch how many amazing doors open. Respect should be given and only lost by action. Treat other people well. Make them feel special. Pay attention to people, really hear them, and they will feel incredible about themselves and you!

Create a culture of respect within your organization. Argue ideas, not the individuals. The media and the government have created a culture where disagreement equals hate. The truth is, in business and leadership, we are required to deal with, lead, and serve all sorts of people, most of whom carry a different set of beliefs and ideologies. In business and leadership, I would rather be rich than right. Everyone is entitled to their beliefs. But once those beliefs and opinions stop you from being able to serve others, your consumer base, or your congregation, those beliefs cease serving you. It is quite possible to disagree with someone, even vehemently, and still respect, value, and lead them. We need to strive to respect all people, all the time. It's hard to get or stay offended by someone you genuinely respect.

"But Ian, what if I don't respect them?" The truth is this: anyone can find faults and shortcomings in other people. You and I are both riddled with a number of our own. It takes leadership and wisdom to search out the great and admirable qualities in another person (and everyone has some of these). Leaders are able to focus on and amplify those qualities. Be a relentless finder of the good in others. When you are constantly conscious of the good in others, it is one of the greatest tools to act as a defense against offense.

GOOD FOR BAD

One of the best ways to improve your life is to return good for bad. There will be no shortage of negativity in life. But when someone does you wrong, hurts you, or throws you under the bus, don't retaliate; go out of your way to bless them. Be good to them, go out of your way to make their lives better. Here's the key: This isn't for them, it's for you!

> **WHEN SOMEONE DOES YOU WRONG, HURTS YOU, OR THROWS YOU UNDER THE BUS, DON'T RETALIATE; GO OUT OF YOUR WAY TO BLESS THEM.**

They don't deserve it! It's not about them. You deserve to go about your day in peace, unencumbered by the weight of offense. It is nearly impossible to be mad at someone you are trying to be good to. Kill them with kindness. People simply won't know how to respond when you return good for bad.

Now, you might say, "It isn't fair. This person really hurt me. You don't know what they did." Here's the key: This is not for them or about them. It's for you. Yes, they hurt you, and yes they were wrong, but if you keep carrying the weight of that offense, it's you that hurts, not them. When you are good to people that haven't been good to you, you become weightless. The offenses roll right off you. They don't stick, they don't keep you mad, and they don't hurt your health and the quality of your work. So, the next time someone does something to you that hurts, bless them, be good to them, let it go, and serve them. When you operate under this principle, you are literally living Jesus' principle of loving your enemies. Anyone can hate their enemy, get even, and seek revenge. Only the most secure, forward, and enlightened leaders can operate truly loving their enemies. Trading good for bad is one of the greatest displays of self-control and self-discipline that exists.

CREATING AN OFFENSE-PROOF CULTURE

Gossip, misinformation, and disinformation are cancer to an organization. There is nothing that kills momentum and trust quite as fast as an offense. One of the greatest creators of offense is gossip. When our human capital is consumed with the latest office news, politics, and agendas, it's hard to focus on much else. Drama is the enemy of productivity. Drama is often created by those who create little else. It brings attention to those whose accolades and accomplishments don't.

> **WHEN YOU ARE GOOD AT CREATING DRAMA, YOU ARE SELDOM GOOD AT MUCH ELSE.**

When you are good at creating drama, you are seldom good at much else. Drama gossip and negativity flourish in the darkness, so shine a light on it and create a gossip-proof culture. One of the best ways to drama-proof your culture is to train on it. Here are a couple of concepts I have continuously deployed for our teams for over 15 years.

NEGATIVES UP

In the hierarchy of command, negative news, concerns, and other sensitive material can't just be ignored. Many organizations and leaders don't want to experience the discomfort of dealing with issues, so they pretend they aren't there, hoping they just resolve themselves. But challenges don't solve themselves, they become greater. Issues have to have someplace to go. We can't pretend it doesn't exist. It must be addressed. The problem is that most of the time, that information is "addressed" and then redistributed by people who have no power to fix it.

In a Negatives Up Team, everyone, everywhere, and at any time, in the organization has a place to bring their concerns. When negatives are not addressed and corrected, they go underground. When it's safe to take negatives and challenges to our superiors without fear of shooting the messenger, it creates a culture where everyone feels they can be heard and are valued. This, simultaneously, assures that the organization has the best possible information about potential issues and threats to the business and culture in real time. When people know there is a place to bring their concerns and grievances, there is little need to share that information with others.

POSITIVES SIDEWAYS AND DOWN

Maintaining a positive and supportive communication path, down rank and side rank within the organization, ensures that negative or potentially negative, critical, or concerning information gets addressed by the right people with the power to solve the problem. Shielding teammates from unnecessary negativity creates a space where the morale of the entity stays high, the concern is low, and positivity and cooperation grow. In this sort of environment, a person is not wasting their time worrying about the information they can't control or business they aren't involved in. When we train everyone on our teams to become immune to offense, gossip, and negativity, it becomes easy for teammates to recognize individuals within the team who aren't living their team's values. This creates herd immunity to the spread of negative, challenging, or potentially destructive information. When this happens, everyone becomes conscious of the quality of their work environment and begin to police their communities with care for the whole.

CAN I QUOTE YOU ON THAT?

A tool I use to train my executive coaching and mastermind-level clients in creating an offense-proof culture is to ask the million-dollar question, "Can I quote you on that?" So many times, when someone has a problem with another person, they take that problem to uninterested third parties instead of trying to reconcile it with the person who caused it.

Here's why: Most people aren't looking for a solution to their problem. Most people are looking for attention they can't get in other ways. They try to character assassinate, gossip, or spread rumors about people instead of producing results. Trying to garner support for their cause and their side of the story, their gossip chips away at the trust of teammates and eventually crushes productivity. Whenever someone in our organization is faced with any form of gossip about another teammate, they are trained to interrupt and immediately ask: "Can I quote you on that?" Proprietors of gossip generally aren't looking for solutions or reconciliation but tend to be seeking attention and validation. If a solution or reconciliation are reached, the power and attention they garner from the drama cease. When confronted with the potential that their stories and allegations are going to be shared back with the party concerned, a gossiper stops in their tracks. After that question is asked, we train our people to ask to bring this issue to the person right then and there. Saying something like, "You know what, I think Steve is just up on the next floor. Why don't we bring this to him right now?" Remember, the gossiper is not looking to *actually* communicate their grievance with the other party for fear of reconciliation. If they were looking for a solution, they would have already brought it to that party. They thrive off the one-sided attention and validation that gossiping brings them. Their worst nightmare is that the complaint may be brought to light and solved, removing their ability to use it any further to get what they seek.

> MOST PEOPLE AREN'T LOOKING FOR A SOLUTION TO THEIR PROBLEM. MOST PEOPLE ARE LOOKING FOR ATTENTION THEY CAN'T GET IN OTHER WAYS.

Gossip thrives only in darkness; light it up and it vaporizes like the wicked witch in the rain. It cannot survive in the light and on the table. The best way to kill it is to teach relational bomb throwers, that their complaints and one-sided stories will not be allowed to remain in the shadows but immediately will be brought to light and put on the table for a solution. This ensures that people take gossip somewhere else or take themselves somewhere else. When others in the community witness people standing up to those who wish to spread negativity, it builds extreme trust within the organization, allowing everyone to have the safety to be themselves, to play right at the line, to make mistakes and grow, knowing that their teammates and coworkers will have zero tolerance for gossip and negativity.

When we create a culture that crushes gossip, misinformation, and negativity at its core, we simultaneously create a culture of great trust and speed, a culture where people are free to take chances, fail, grow and learn, and press the limits.

CELEBRATING SUCCESS

Immature leaders in business are threatened by the success of others around them. They are okay with others succeeding, just not as much as them. Early in our careers, we might see people who were winning and immediately try to discount their victories. I, personally, would find flaws in what the people ahead of me were doing and discredit their success, as if in some way, it would make my success look even better. This sort of thinking is part of a scarcity mindset. For them to be more successful, then I must be less successful. In this mindset, we ultimately see success as finite and limited. As I have grown as a leader, I have come to understand that many people can simultaneously be wildly successful. And when we genuinely celebrate the success of others, we can learn from them. When we minimize the leader, we minimize their message. Instead of cheapening the successes of those achieving around you, celebrate them. When you do that, you pass the test. When you show others around you that you are not consumed or overtaken by their success, it opens you up to even more success. Celebrating successes is part of an offense-proof culture.

CATCH YOUR PEOPLE IN THE ACT (OF DOING SOMETHING RIGHT)

What gets recognized, gets repeated. People have a deep desire and fundamental need for respect and recognition. Everyone wants attention. People achieve more consistently under a spirit of approval than they do under a spirit of criticism. Most people are only recognized by their superiors, peers, or spouse when something goes wrong. To offense proof your culture, make it a habit to catch people in the act of doing something right. Make an example of what they did and why it's important. When others see the behaviors that are recognized, they subconsciously begin to desire to emulate those behaviors and obtain that same praise for themselves.

WHAT GETS RECOGNIZED, GETS REPEATED.

When we build a culture of recognition and praise, we create a system where people know how to positively and productively fill their need for respect and recognition. Think about a child acting out. You may have children. If you do, you will probably recognize this tendency right away. If you don't have children, at some point in your life, you have witnessed this behavior in other people's children. Many times, when a child is starved for attention, they will begin to act out in a plethora of different ways, getting in trouble at school, getting in fights at home, or maybe drastically changing their appearance. Many times, these behaviors are the negative expression of the need for attention and recognition. Because the child doesn't know how to obtain these desires through positive means, they will attempt to fulfill them through negative ones. This behavior is visible in adults too. Remember, adults are just children in grown-up bodies. Their primal needs for acceptance, attention, approval, and recognition remain very much intact. When the people on your team, in your church, or on your staff don't see clear and predictable positive ways to meet their needs for attention and approval, they will look for other ways to meet these needs. When people don't have constructive ways to be recognized and affirmed, they will create destructive means for attaining these things.

When you are full from Thanksgiving dinner, you aren't in a rush to run out to McDonald's and crush a Big Mac. In the same way, when people are full of positive praise and recognition, they aren't lined up to meet those needs in potentially harmful or negative ways. Always remember this: large problems start small. Small issues, unaddressed and left to fester, make big issues … Recognize the small stuff, and the big stuff takes care of itself.

RECOGNIZE THE SMALL STUFF, AND THE BIG STUFF TAKES CARE OF ITSELF.

EDIFICATION—A LOST ART

Part of offense-proofing your culture is creating a positive and uplifting high-trust environment.

Today, we are taught to discredit and vilify those who are further ahead of us. But here's the truth—tearing others down won't make us stand any taller. Any fool can complain and criticize, and most do. Great leaders criticize sometimes too, but get this key: *criticize in private and praise in public*. The art of public praise is called edification. Edification is about building those up around you publicly. I'm a firm believer you should talk behind everybody's back about *all of the good* you know of them. When we look for the good in others, and take a role in actively sharing and promoting that to other people, we edify our teams and leaders. Teams operate at the speed of trust. To create a climate of trust, create a culture of edification.

Diseases that grow in the darkness stand no chance in the sunlight. Edification shines a light across your entire organization. Nothing is more common than someone with a negative opinion of others who's willing to share that with you. Nothing is more uncommon than someone who goes out of their way to make others look good. When you edify others, you build relational capital, both with the people you are edifying and the people you are sharing that edification with. They see you as someone who is looking out for the good of others and instantly become more comfortable with you. They tend to believe that because you talk that way about one person, you may talk that way about them too. This goes both ways, by the way. When you talk poorly behind others' backs, the people who experience that will ultimately expect you to do that to them one day as well. Edification is one of the great tools for war against the onset of offense. When our minds and hearts and mouths are consumed with the good in other people, it's hard to be consumed by their flaws.

RELATIONSHIP ACCOUNTS

This idea is not a new idea. It has been around for a long time, and yet, I've witnessed so few people using it, so it is worth a discussion here. The idea of relationship bank accounts equates relationships with the deposit and withdrawal system of accounts at a bank. The more money you put into the account, the larger the balance you have. Withdrawals out of the account reduce the balance. If enough withdrawals occur, the account can go into the negative.

This, in many ways, is how our relationships work. When we do something to strengthen the relationship, we have made a "deposit". It could be a thoughtful gesture, helping out, defending that person, being there for them, picking up the tab, or a number of other relationship positives. The more these occur, the higher the balance is in that relationship account.

Most of us are unaware of the balances of the accounts in our relationships. This is a leading cause of frustration and offense within our relationships. When a withdrawal that is larger than the available balance occurs, the relationship hits a patch of friction. If the overdraw is substantial enough, it can permanently close that account. Withdrawals occur when something is asked of someone. No matter how large or small, any unreciprocated effort such as, can you cover my shift, pick me up from the airport, cover for me, lend me a few bucks, etc., are all forms of relationship withdrawal. Emotional conversations, favors, and other things are all withdrawals from the relationship account. Since most people are unaware of the balances in their accounts and are not proactively depositing into them, the likelihood to overdraw them is high.

When we ask for more from someone than we have given to them, offense occurs. One of the greatest ways to become offense-proof is to mind the quality and quantity of relationship deposits. Here are a couple of ideas to help you maintain millions in those relationship accounts.

1. Go out of your way. It doesn't take long to hold the door, pick up the tab on lunch, or send a card or encouraging email. These things are not costly or time-consuming, but they do require our focus to shift from ourselves to others. The larger the balances we can accumulate, the larger the withdrawals we may be able to make at some point in the future without bankrupting the account.

2. Practice self-filling. One of the surest ways to become unoffendable is to

practice filling your own bank account. When your account is full, it's less likely you will need to take a withdrawal from someone else's account. You don't need to wait for others to fill your account, you can fill it yourself. Self-development, positive affirmation, constructive self-talk, gratitude, practice, a strong sense of identity, and creating the habit of seeing the best in others are all ways to keep your own

WE WILL NEVER HAVE A POSITIVE LIFE WITH A NEGATIVE ATTITUDE.

tank full. When you do this, when the trials and tests of life eventually come, as they always do, you won't be drawn into the negative when other people take withdrawals on your time, energy, money, and patience.

At the end of the day, our attitude is our responsibility. We will never have a positive life with a negative attitude. Offense-proofing our lives and cultivating the capacity for enthusiasm will be two of the best ways to ensure a stable, consistent, predictably positive attitude.

CHAPTER 8

HEART

heart

/härt/

noun

1. the central or innermost part of something.

———

*"There ain't nobody ever designed a test, nor will they
design a test, that can measure the heart of a man or woman."*
Art Williams

Y ou win with your heart, not with your head. There are a million great ideas out there, but heart is what makes them happen. Heart gives us the power to push through amidst fierce competition, strenuous regulation, and dozens of other factors that kill fledgling ideas before launching. A decided heart finds a way. An undecided heart finds an excuse. It's about how badly you want your dream. How bad do you want it? Are you all in? Does your dream burn fiercely inside of you? Does it keep you up at night and wake you up in the morning? When it comes to leadership, whether at home, in your church, or in the boardroom, heart trumps facts every day of the week.

> **A DECIDED HEART FINDS A WAY. AN UNDECIDED HEART FINDS AN EXCUSE.**

Let's look at the three sorts of heart-driven (or lack thereof) leaders.

1. THE EMOTIONALLY DISCONNECTED

The "It Would Be Nice" leader. It would be nice to win, but it's okay if I don't.

These are the people that are intrigued by the accolades of success but just don't really believe that it's going to happen for them. They don't put in the work, they don't grind it out, and they don't fight for what they want. They are, in a word, apathetic, which is the way most people in the world live. They've set up permanent residence in "it must be nice-ville." They'd love to have their goals and dreams, but they're not gonna kill themselves to get it. They would love a life of meaning, purpose, and significance if someone would just kindly throw it in their lap. But when the struggle hits, when every day is a battle just to stay afloat, they hit the eject button for a safer but insignificant existence. These people like the idea of success but don't want the responsibilities of it. Winners take it personally, these sorts of leaders take nothing personally.

2. THE EMOTIONALLY INCONSISTENT

This group of leaders will pay a price for a period of time. They're all-in while it's interesting, easy, or fun. They love it, while they're being recognized, while it's not asking more of them than they were originally willing to pay. When it gets costly, or time-consuming, or demands more of them than they are willing to pay, they often bail. But the champion will pay the price. Any price.

> **SIGNIFICANT SUCCESS DEMANDS THAT THE PRICE BE PAID UPFRONT AND IN FULL.**

The problem with this group is they want to choose the price they are willing to pay, and that's not how success works. Success never goes on sale. Significant success demands that the price be paid upfront and in full. It is never at a discount, and it's never negotiable. Success is a lot like wrestling a gorilla: You stop when the gorilla is tired, not when you are. This group is unwilling to make the total commitment necessary to secure the goal. The price of success is the price it demands, and it takes how long it takes. You can't force those two things. They want their dream, as long as it happens on their timetable. Heart is about loving the game more than the outcome. It's about loving the process more than the prize. That's why you can't beat someone with heart. They aren't deterred by what you are deterred by. THEY WANT IT BAD! How bad do you want it?

3. THE WARRIOR

The third group of leaders are warriors. Some people were born for the fight; they were literally created to fight, conquer, and fight again, on some other valiant conquest. They leave it all on the field, and they never stop at the finish line. To a warrior, the finish line is just a mile marker. The starting line of the next conquest. They are never finished. They love the hard battle. They want to be great. Winning is good, but greatness is better. They aren't deterred by obstacles and failures. They are dialed in on the vision at hand. Obstacles are what you see

TO A WARRIOR, THE FINISH LINE IS JUST A MILE MARKER.

when you take your eyes off the goal. The heart-driven leader's eyes, mind, and soul are always focused on the goal. Heart is the great equalizer; it overcomes what we lack in skill, connections, or resources. Set yourself on fire and people will come from miles to watch you burn. People are attracted to the authenticity and raw emotion of a leader who's playing with heart. We can all feel it when someone is just there for the money, the title, or the influence. It's when we find a leader that really leads with heart, that burns with vision, that our hearts are captivated. People can't help but be attracted to that sort of leader. When the vision resides only at the conscious level, as adversities arise and the costs become apparent, the logic-driven leader eventually begins to back off. The heart-driven leader pays no attention to the cost. They will spend their whole life gladly paying for it. The vision is part of them, it's who they are, and they will die for that cause.

How do we become heart-driven leaders?

ENGAGE A COMPELLING "WHY"

WHEN THE WHY IS CLEAR, THE HOW-TO WILL APPEAR.

When the why is clear, the how-to will appear. Get clear on what you want, why you want it, and who will benefit from it. When you know why, you can endure almost any how. Our why's, to be effective, need to be three things.

1. Clear—"Where there is no vision, the people perish" (Prov. 29:18, KJV). Most people in life don't know what they want or why they want it. When you don't know where you're going, any path will get you there.

2. Compelling—Your why needs to mean something to you. Most people lie about their why. If it doesn't matter to you, it won't move you.

3. Connected—You must believe that you're why is achievable for you.

It's okay to be all-in. Let me give you permission to win, to dominate, to play wide open. When we were kids, and we get excited about something, a new sport, becoming a famous pop star, or changing the medical profession, many times, we are told not to get our hopes up. Well-meaning but limited people try to discourage us. But understand this: those are their limits, not yours. When we go all-in on something, people who have given up on their dreams try to protect us, afraid that like them, we won't make it. But their limits are not our limits. Over time, if we aren't careful, we can begin to succumb to these limits and

IT'S OKAY TO BE ALL-IN.

play it safe. We never really go all-in. We never really engage. And while we may be protected from temporary defeats, we are permanently barred from world-changing wins. It's time to scrap that. Get your hopes up! Put your heart in it. Go all-in. Yes, it hurts from time to time when we lose, when we fail, when we stop short, or take a tough loss. But to a person playing with heart, that failure is never final. They will always fight another fight. Heart-based leaders don't just win more often, but they enjoy their wins, are present in the moment, and value the people around them on the journey.

THE SEVEN WHYS

One of the best ways to discover your clear, compelling, and connected "why" is to go through an exercise I call "The Seven Whys."

Writer Mark Twain famously said, "I can teach anybody how to get what they want out of life. The problem is that I can't find anybody who can tell me what they want."[20]

The Seven Whys is an exercise in clarity I love to use when refocusing a leader playing below their potential. A common phrase in the sales and leadership businesses is that you must know the why that makes you cry. It's a statement used to describe the deep emotional connection to why you are doing what you are doing. But the truth is, most people don't really know what they want or why they want it. They've never stopped to think about it long enough to create the clarity needed for massive success. The road to your dreams is full of clearly marked exits to lesser dreams. Clarity and connection are what give a leader the power to stay focused on the one true why and the one real path. So, here are The Seven Whys:

1. *Why* do you want what you want? Stop now and take a minute to write out a one to two sentence answer. Seriously, stop reading and do this … It needs to be clear and concise, and it may prove more difficult than you initially anticipate. It's okay. Stay with it until you get that sentence or two down about why it matters to you to accomplish what you're striving for. Once you have that sentence written, now the real work begins.

2. *Why* is that sentence important to you?

3. *Why* does that matter? What does it really mean to you? Take a few minutes and write the answer to that question. Now, you've got a couple of sentences written down about why your dream or vision matters to you.

4. Now, ask yourself *why* that means something to you. Take a few minutes and answer.

5. Now, *why* is that important? Again, write this down.

6. *Why* does that matter to the people that are important to you? Write your answer.

7. And lastly, why is it important to the world at large?

If you're willing to take the time to truthfully and deeply answer these questions, you have successfully engaged your heart in your venture. You know deeply and clearly why what you're doing matters to you, to the people around you, and to the world at large.

Play with heart—nobody outworks you, and nobody loves it like you … Be that kid on the team who maybe wasn't the most talented but just outworked everyone else on the field. The grind is the kid who fought just to play. When you play with your heart, you let nothing deny you from your dream. You understand there's always a way. Sometimes, you have to find it, and sometimes you have to make it, but there's always a way. See, anybody can play hard and give it their best when momentum is on their side, but it's when the momentum shifts and you're flat and you don't see a way, but you keep fighting. In fact, you're not only to keep fighting, but you take your fight to a new level, to an unprecedented place where nobody can keep up with you, and all you can focus on is finishing the job. In every great battle, and every great game, and every great head-to-head, somebody always gives up first. The heart-driven leader never says die.

> **THE HEART-DRIVEN LEADER NEVER SAYS DIE.**

ALIGNMENT

One of the biggest components of playing with your heart, all of the time, is to create an alignment between your brain and your emotion. Imagine a bathroom sink with water flowing out into the sink below. The water flows uninhibited until stopped by the perpendicular faucet handle. The handle actually creates misalignment and stops the flow of water. In the same way, alignment between your conscious and subconscious acts as the faucet of results in your life. When alignment is present, it flows. Your thinking and beliefs will either create a flow of success or a stoppage of achievement in your life. Are your stated goals and dreams and your deepest-held subconscious beliefs in alignment? For many people, the secret to their "would-be" success lies in the power of alignment. Alignment consists of two components:

1. the conscious thought processes

2. our subconscious belief systems

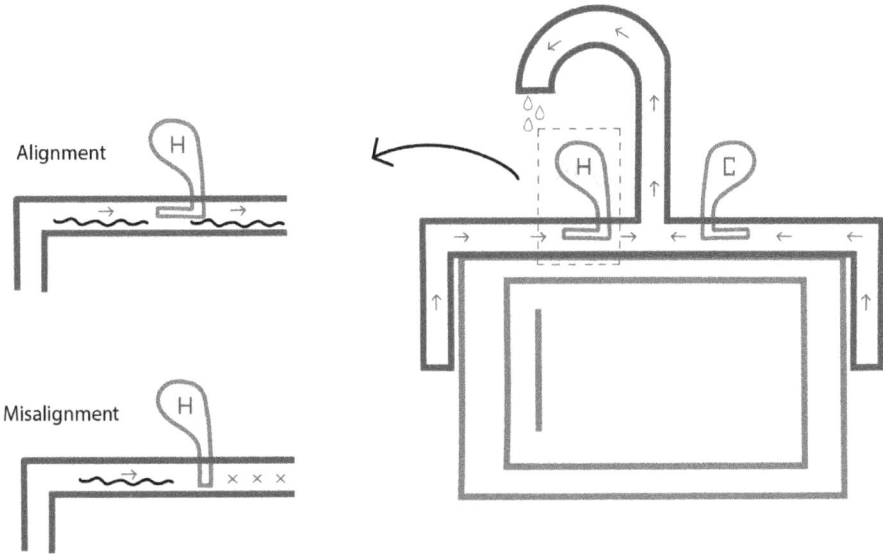

In other words, do our thoughts and beliefs line up? Does what we say we want and what we deeply believe we want, align? Many times, we are unaware of our subconscious belief systems. Often, they are put there years or even decades earlier by well-meaning but potentially unqualified donors. These belief systems combine to create our core operating system. They are filters through which every action passes. Many times, people find themselves knowing what to do but not doing it. Their thought process is correct; they've correctly and clearly identified what steps they need to take, but, yet, find it challenging to consistently act on them, or sometimes to even act at all. They know how to take the steps, but they don't do it. What causes this breakdown between thought and action? Let's take a look back at the TBAR example from earlier in the book.

Thought is conscious. It's active. A thought that is held long enough, and repeated often and vividly enough, eventually moves from the conscious into the subconscious, where they are stored and combined into new and unique belief systems. Results flow easily and almost effortlessly to those whose conscious thought processes and subconscious belief systems are in alignment. When what we think and what we believe are lined up, it's easy for us to take action. When they're not, we find ourselves stuck in a pattern of stagnation and frustration, knowing what we want but finding ourselves unwilling to take action. Action is the byproduct of our belief system. When our belief system is not in alignment with our thinking, the thought never makes its way to the action phase of the formula (see picture below). The belief system acts as that faucet stopper, stopping the flow of energy from thought to belief, and eventually, into action and, ultimately, result.

THOUGHTS ➤ BELIEFS ➤ ACTIONS ➤ RESULTS

Satisfaction, enjoyment, happiness, and success are all byproducts of alignment. When your beliefs, values, and principles move you in the same direction, you are in alignment. In my previous book *BYPRODUCT*, I discuss the idea that all natural actions are the byproduct of the beliefs that created them. When this is naturally occurring, we operate from a foundation of heart. However, many of us spend most of our lives taking actions required of us by others at work, school, or in our careers that aren't the natural outcome of our beliefs and values. When the beliefs and values we hold are not in line with the actions being taken, we become misaligned. When we're out of alignment, we experience an array of negative emotions ranging from stress to guilt to just plain negativity and a sense of unrest or lack of well-being. This is exactly why so many people feel stress and pressure and are unhappy in their careers. It's because there is a misalignment between what's important to them and what they are being required to do. For example, an employee values family time but is consistently working overtime to catch up with a never-ending stream of deadlines at work. No matter how much success that person has at work, they are out of alignment with what they truly value. This eventually causes stress and unhappiness. When we are out of alignment but acting under the compulsion of our responsibilities, the outcome will always be unhappy, unfulfilled, and unproductive. We are disconnected from our hearts.

Who are you? What do you want? Where are you going, and what values will guide you on your journey? You can have it all if you are willing to discover what "all" really means and forge an authentic path forward. You must travel your path or the destination you arrive at, won't be yours.

Misalignment often manifests as a lack of action or productivity. Have you ever known exactly what you had to do but it seemed as though you were paralyzed? Take two entrepreneurs, for example. Both are working for the same opportunity, and both with similar desires; both make the tough COMMITMENTS; both experience the ups and downs of starting a business.

Entrepreneur A has a growth mindset. He believes all things are learnable, and he sees obstacles as evidence of a deficiency. His belief says that with enough time and effort, that deficiency would be correctable. He's all in.

Entrepreneur B has a fixed mindset. She sees obstacles as proof that she, as a person, isn't good enough. Challenges mean she probably isn't cut out for the gig, and she directs her efforts to find something easier and more naturally suited for her.

Entrepreneur A is operating in alignment. His thinking (goals) beliefs and actions are all moving in the same direction. He thinks the venture will be worth it. He expects obstacles along the way, he believes that challenges are normal and that he is capable of handling them. When they arise, he buckles down, focuses like mad, and bursts through them to the other side. The alignment between his thinking and beliefs creates the action that manifests success.

Entrepreneur B, on the other hand, wants the outcome but isn't sure she is capable of attaining it. She thinks the venture will be worth it but doesn't expect obstacles along the way. She erroneously believes that it will take less time and require less effort than it actually does. When this belief is challenged, instead of looking for solutions, she begins to doubt herself: *Maybe I'm just not good at sales. Maybe I'm just not good with people* ... etc. Entrepreneur B is out of alignment. Her thinking says go but her belief system says stay. With this misalignment in place, the necessary effort to overcome the challenge and succeed almost never occurs. People with heart never give up; people lacking heart always give up ... eventually.

This misalignment is also visible in the executive who strongly values people and integrity but is under immense pressure from the board to cut people and corners to save money. He may act on it out of duty and responsibility to the position, but inside, personally, there is a war. It's a war of misalignment. The job that used to bring passion and excitement becomes stressful and burdensome. The emotional load of constantly acting against your deepest beliefs and values eventually creates burnout and deep emptiness.

A lack of heart is best characterized by chronic inaction. Without internal alignment, we never get around to doing much. Our big dreams and desires will lie unfulfilled and unfinished, hidden behind the burdens of worry, fear, and doubt. Overthinking and overanalyzing are internal alignment miscalculations. We're always wrestling with ourselves, doubting ourselves, confused, and lacking clarity when we are not aligned internally. What we say we want and what we *actually* want need to be one and the same. Until they are, we're doomed to go round and round in circles of stress, anxiety, and underachievement. Heart is the key that opens the door to success; misalignment is the key that locks it.

CHAPTER 9

RELENTESS

re·lent·less
/rə'len(t)ləs/

adjective

1. oppressively constant; incessant.

In 2008, I was calling through a list of prospects, much like I did every day for two years. I was circling back to people that I'd contacted previously. I called a man I had spoken with a few times before. Up until that point, he had been unwilling to give me an appointment, but I called him again, making my quarterly rounds. We chatted for a couple of minutes. In the end, he refused to grant me an appointment again, but this time, he left me with something that changed my life. He said in a worn-out sigh, "You are relentless, aren't you?" I think he meant it half as a complement and half as a jab, but

> **ONLY WHEN ONE REFUSES TO QUIT WILL EFFORT FULLY RELEASE ITS REWARD.**

I took it for what it was worth. I am relentless. I am unceasing and unwavering. I couldn't get that word out of my mind for the rest of the day. That night, I went home and talked to my wife, and we decided we would name our agency Team Relentless; we would take what somebody had meant as a jab and use it as a rallying cry. I've built mansions out of the bricks other people have thrown at me. That day, Relentless was born. Relentless wasn't just what we did, it was who we were. So much of winning is hanging on after everyone else has called it quits. When everyone else is throwing in the towel, people who are *relentless* are just getting started.

> **MOST PEOPLE, MOST OF THE TIME, ARE PLAYING NOT TO LOSE. SOME PEOPLE PLAY TO WIN. BUT RELENTLESS IS PLAYING FOR TOTAL DOMINATION.**

Only when one refuses to quit will effort fully release its reward. Staying in the game is essential to any victory, but consistent victory, dynastic victory, and total dominance-type victory require a lot more than staying in the game, it requires a certain relentlessness; a drive to push yourself and your boundaries further than anyone else could possibly ask you to push. It's about taking new ground, becoming the best, making everyone else chase you, and redefining the game. Most people, most of the time, are playing not to lose. Some people play to win. But relentless is playing for total domination. Relentless is about the ability to fall over and over and over but never lose the fire inside for what you really want. It's that insatiable hunger and drive that pushes you further and faster than everyone around you. Relentless is about the pursuit. It's an all-out total focus. It's about hammering that goal over and over and over until it has no choice but to finally submit to your sheer determination. It's about wanting it so bad you don't rest until it's done. Complete. Finished.

But, even after it's done, you don't celebrate; you already have the next target locked in and ready to attack. Think about a child in a toy store who wants that certain toy more than life itself. They start by asking. After a few Nos, they change their strategy and try to help you rationalize why you should get it for them. They have been good. Their grades have been improving, and they will give you some of their money when you get home. The strategy then shifts again. It moves from logic to the emotional realm. I need that toy; everyone else has one. If I don't have it, I'll be a loser, and all the other kids will think I'm a maniac … From emotional arguments, they then move into mild tantrum mode, followed by full tantrum mode, and they complete the round with full-blown demon mode. They are getting that toy or everyone within ear distance is going to know about it.

School civilized us. It taught us to fit in at all costs. We are taught not to stand out and to not pursue what we really want out of fear that we will be judged, or worse, left out. That might work for keeping an orderly classroom, but life is a jungle. In that jungle, you need a killer instinct. We don't get what we want in life or what we would love to have; we get what we fight for, period. What is worth fighting for in your life? Your family? Your health? Your spouse? Your children? Your dreams? Are you fighting for it? Are you taking ground, at all costs?

Relentless is accepting only results, no excuses. Relentless is about showing up every day and leaving it all on the field. One thing that relentless is *not*, is celebrating too soon. Most people celebrate too soon and for too long. Relentless is about getting back to work. It's about redefining the game, the industry, and total dominance. It's about having such a white-hot desire to win and to dominate, no one has to hold you accountable. Nobody has to give you goals, or targets, or follow up with you. You just do it. Every day, you do what you need to do, when you need to do it, because that's who you are. You don't expect applause and pats on the back for bringing your best. You expect it from yourself and others. Today, we have a creed built around the name Relentless. It embodies the incredible achievements that our team made in that industry. At the beginning of every training, these agents would say The Relentless Creed together. They are more than words; they are a way of life. I hope it inspires you to be relentless.

THE RELENTLESS CREED

I am relentless.

I am a competitor.

I do what others won't, so I can have what others don't.

I will pay the price and expect to win.

My future is bright.

I am a champion.

COMPETITION

In the heart of every relentless person runs an insatiable drive to compete. Being relentless is about being a warrior at heart. In every great battle, one side eventually gives up; it better not be you. In every great challenge, whether it be a military battle or your favorite football team going head-to-head, one side eventually gives in. Inside every human being is a desire to compete, to win, and to grow. It's innate and inborn; it is part of our very DNA. Being relentless is about being a competitor. Since the beginning of recorded time, humans have been infatuated with competition. From the ancient Olympic games, to the gladiators in the Colosseum of Rome, to the vast battles for land and territory, competition is woven, inseparably, into the fabric of the human heart.

IN THE HEART OF EVERY RELENTLESS PERSON RUNS AN INSATIABLE DRIVE TO COMPETE.

Everything in life, like it or not, is a competition. We compete to make the team and to stay on the team. We compete to win our spouses, and we compete to keep them. We compete for our job, and we compete to keep it. It doesn't matter if you like it or not, you're competing all of the time, so you might as well get great at it. The competition calls the best out of us.

It pushes us to levels that, without it, we would never reach. It forces us to finally put our skills and practice to the test and to see where we stand.

EVERYTHING IN LIFE, LIKE IT OR NOT, IS A COMPETITION.

Every intersection of our life is marked by competition, and yet, today, the very idea of competition is looked down upon. "Not everything is a contest; just play for fun," they say. The problem with this idea is that competing and having fun are only mutually exclusive for losers. This idea couldn't be further from the truth. Competing is, in and of itself, fun. The thrill of the fight, the surge of the chase, the worthy opponent, and the moments of clarity in the defining seconds of the game are all things that drive human emotion and achievement. As the shot clock ticks down, our internal furnace fires up. Winners learn to, not only embrace competition, but to create it, using competition as a force to drive themselves to perform at the highest levels. One of the secrets of super achievers is their ability to create a competition out of mundane and monotonous tasks that create success. It's the salesperson who competes against themselves, trying to set more appointments this hour than they did the last. It's the pastor who sets the goal of having 2000 people at this Easter Sunday service and drives the team and congregation to hit that target.

> **WINNERS LOVE THE COMPETITION. THEY SEEK IT OUT. THEY LOVE THE HARD BATTLE.**

It's the major leaguer, trash-talking his friend on the other team, during the press conference after game 6 of the World Series. They are all looking for that little extra edge, that special something that sets them apart and ignites that raw emotion and heart power to battle through to victory. Every super achiever understands the power of competition.

Competition draws a crowd. Everyone wants to see the players play. By leveraging competition to create an audience, we leave a deeply-rooted, emotional desire for respect and recognition, allowing us to push past what might have held us back in private to play at our very best. Losing is one thing; losing in front of millions of people is quite another. While you may not be playing on the biggest field in the world, wherever you are competing, the public pressure of the loss is a powerful motivator for performance. "I don't like competition" is code for, "I don't want others to see how little I have produced or mastered." Winners love the competition. They seek it out. They love the hard battle. If competition is such a powerful driving force for achievement, why has society steadily drifted away from it?

One reason competition and the drive to compete have slowed in recent years is that many find themselves competing in a game that they are designed to lose. It's like the opposing team for the Harlem Globetrotters; every single game they have ever played or will ever play is a loss, designed and destined before the beginning of time. We are wired to win. After constant and consistent losses, the players on the opposing team have to be rotated out. We are not designed to play in games where we have no chance to win. We thrive off the possibility. We can't thrive where the losses are pre-arranged for us. Yet, that is exactly what so many experience in the real world. Even when they win, they're losing.

Think about the straight-A student that followed the path laid out for them, perfectly. They went to school, got good grades, got into a great school, and got a good job working for a prestigious company. They did everything right. On the outside, it looks like a win, but their health is failing after years of stress and poor eating. Their marriage is suffering from long hours at work. They missed their kids growing up while climbing the corporate ladder, and yet, they are stuck in a holding pattern, waiting for the person above them to quit or die for their next promotion. The money is okay, but they are still in debt; they stay up at night worrying about the impending retirement and the sorry state of their 401k. Does this sound familiar?

This is the corporate globetrotter game that 10s of millions have played and are playing, designed from inception for you to lose and the corporation to win. They get the very best of our lifetime and creativity, and we get an income, rented out in 2-week periods in return. After decades of watching those around them experience this loss, in spite of every effort to win, the economic playing field has shifted, and competing to win has all but disappeared, and along with it, corporate loyalty. If you can't win, why play the game?

The mindset of today's employees is shifting. They go from employer to employer, taking as much as they can out of the deal before they leave for the next one, not concerned with playing to win any longer, but simply taking the low-hanging fruit and moving on to the next tree. So many have competed for so long, only to find that winning was a mirage. The bigger house, the bigger car, the more prestigious title, only to find that when they got there, it wasn't what they thought it would be.

Another factor contributing to the diminishment of competition is the pain of losing. If you don't compete, you can't lose, right? When we compete, we are faced with the prospect of losing. While most people let the loss define them, winners let the loss *refine them*. Relentless people understand that losing is a necessary and unavoidable part of winning. In fact, winners lose more often and in far greater ways than most losers do. A loser loses and thinks: I am a loser. A winner loses and says: Here's an area of deficiency I need to correct. When we avoid competition, we also avoid the impending potential of a loss. The irony is, by avoiding the potential of losing, we lock in sure losses to the quality of our life. Winners know that losing is a part of the game, and it makes the win that much sweeter.

It's the thrill of victory and the agony of defeat. A great competitor always wants to play a worthy opponent. They know true greatness is only really released in the fire of the competitive battle.

LIFE KEEPS SCORE

Whether you like it or not, the game of life is keeping score. The quality of your health, a scoreboard. The size of your bank account, a scoreboard. The richness of your relationships, a scoreboard. Your spiritual well-being, a scoreboard. Whether we like it or not, or want to participate in it or not, life is keeping score. How are you doing in the game of life? Like weekend warriors, average people are content just playing the game, kicking the ball around a bit, and then calling it a day. Truly relentless people don't just play the game, they love the game, and they love the scoreboard because it shows them where they fit in that game.

> **WHETHER YOU LIKE IT OR NOT, THE GAME OF LIFE IS KEEPING SCORE.**

HOW TO DEVELOP A COMPETITOR'S SPIRIT

1. It starts with understanding that competition is productive—It's not always pleasant, but it is very productive. The pressure of the competition takes us further and faster than we could have taken ourselves. The greats love the hard battle, they want to play against a worthy competitor.

2. Find a record and hunt it down—Sometimes competition isn't against someone else. Sometimes, it's against a standard or a record. Sometimes, it's against yourself. One of the greatest tools an ultra-competitor will develop is the ability

to turn anything into a competition. When we're competing, the grind becomes fun; competition gives purpose to the monotony of practice. Whatever you're competing against, rest assured, it's making you tougher, stronger, and more fierce than you could ever imagine.

3. Find an adversary—An army isn't needed without an enemy. The team in the wrong-colored jersey can have an incredible effect on productivity and results. Many people will play much harder for the team than for themselves. They will battle for a cause that captivates them. Find an enemy, even if you have to create one. The emotional connection to the competition will move you miles further than you would have gone without it. Competition against a worthy adversary takes the monotony of success and gives it a purpose. In John Wooden's book, *They Call Me Coach*, he talks about his pyramid of success.[21] Atop the pyramid is the cornerstone of Competitive Greatness, or what he calls the love of the hard battle. Relentless people don't just want to play the game, they want to play the game against a worthy competitor.

4. Make it PUBLIC—Don't be a secret agent. Make your contest public. Like a boxer face-to-face with his opponent in front of the lights and cameras, public pressure augments performance like almost nothing else. Losing is one thing, losing in front of millions of people is quite another. Public competition creates a higher emotional engagement in the outcome. What we might have been tempted to settle with privately, we are forced to battle for publicly.

5. The win-loss reward punishment—Competition, like any mindset, becomes stronger the more it is reinforced. A great way to cultivate a competitive culture is to tie rewards and punishments to measurable performances. When you do this, you create internal competition for the attainment or avoidance of something. Stop and think about the average company's compensation structure. Tied generally to tenure or other non-performance-related metrics, this frustrates high performers and causes them to leave for greener pastures, while rewarding those who can simply outlast the rest. Most people reward themselves for a job not done. They just buy what they want, when they want, on credit, whether or not they have done anything to earn it. But there is a better way! When you delay the gratification until successfully completing a goal, two things happen:

(1) rising pressure and (2) desire for the reward begins to occupy more emotional space. When we reward ourselves arbitrarily, we teach ourselves that winning and work ethic are not important. When gratification is delayed until the win, we begin to tie winning, emotionally, with reward. Today, with easy credit, you can feel like a winner, without actually winning.

Think about video games, or as I like to call them, electronic income reducers. One of the reasons they're so addicting is because they release the same sort of chemical endorphin when you win a video game as when you have a major win in real life. The person playing the video game, emotionally, has the reward of having a great life achievement, although, they have achieved absolutely nothing. Fat and happy from the feeling of achievement, there's no need to go out into the real world and actually achieve. Similarly, when we buy whatever we want, whenever we want, we lose the capacity to push ourselves into action in the pursuit of reward. In the early years of my business career, I tied rewards to each $50,000 increase in income I achieved. After about $500,000 in annual income, most things, within reason, I could purchase whenever I wanted. But, I specifically didn't; I put off making large purchases until I hit the next $50,000 income goal. That forced me to continue to grow my income into the seven figures

> **MOST PEOPLE ARE COMFORTABLE, AND COMFORT KILLS … AT LEAST, WHEN IT COMES TO SUCCESS.**

and beyond. Most people are comfortable, and comfort kills … at least, when it comes to success. Healthy competition brings out the best in every competitor. You either learn to compete or you learn to be satisfied with the leftovers.

PERSEVERANCE

Relentless isn't a talent business, it's a tenacity business. Be like the postage stamp. It's usefulness consists of its ability to stick to something until it gets there. Many times,

> **SUCCESS IS JUST A MATTER OF HOLDING ON AFTER EVERYBODY ELSE LETS GO.**

success is just a matter of holding on after everybody else lets go. Perseverance is the measure of how long you can endure disappointment on the way to great success. So much of success is about continuing on beyond where everyone else stops. While everyone else gives their dreams six months or a year, truly relentless people give it a lifetime. Many times in life, the final test you have to pass is answering the question of how badly do you want this? The fact is, no matter what obstacle you talk about, whether it's curing an incurable disease, sending people to the moon, or creating a world-changing technology, it's hard for anything to forever withstand the constantly applied force of the human will.

> **WHILE EVERYONE ELSE GIVES THEIR DREAMS SIX MONTHS OR A YEAR, TRULY RELENTLESS PEOPLE GIVE IT A LIFETIME.**

Today, it's common for us to move on from one idea to the next, one job to the next, one ministry to the next, and one relationship to the next. It's as if, as soon as we are hit with adversity, we pack up the tent and go home. Our culture teaches us if it's not easy, it's not something for us to pursue. They tell us we should find something we love, follow happiness, and always do you.

The problem with this ideology is twofold. First, it is self-centric. We are the center of the universe in this ideology. Whatever doesn't make us happy, whatever whim our emotions move us to, that's where we need to go. The problem is, it's not how the world works. We've got to understand that for life to be rich and rewarding, we must live in community and alignment with others and our surroundings.

Additionally, it is an ideology that places a great deal of emphasis on emotion. Feelings are liars, and they're terrible leaders. We're not always going to feel like doing what we need to do. We won't always feel in love with our spouse. We won't always love our work, and putting in a grueling workout isn't fun.

> **REAL PROGRESS IS NEVER EASY.**

Learning a new skill and playing at the point of failure isn't comfortable. But there's no growth in the familiar. There is no leadership in the comfortable. REAL PROGRESS is *NEVER* EASY. Actual progress, something that has never been done before, isn't easy. A new solution has not been found before because it isn't easy. The world's greatest problems, and their greatest rewards, will never be easy to solve and achieve. We need to stop looking for easy and start looking for things worth our very best; our very best effort, our very best commitment, and our very best thinking. It's about the relentless

WE NEED TO STOP LOOKING FOR EASY AND START LOOKING FOR THINGS WORTH OUR VERY BEST

hammering against what is, to create what will be. Tenacity is that force. It's the force allowing us to continue to assault our status quo in the pursuit of who and what we are supposed to become.

KEEP GOING

We are not called to comfort, we are called to *significance*. Is it a worthy cause? Is it a need? Will it improve the world? These questions must be answered when we decide which endeavors in life require tenacity. Not everything we do warrants completion. But, if it does, we better finish that job.

Some of us have become professionals at succeeding at things that don't matter. We put in countless hours of emotion and endless streams of money moving things that don't move the needle. Sometimes, it doesn't make sense to approach something with tenacity.

WE ARE NOT CALLED TO COMFORT, WE ARE CALLED TO SIGNIFICANCE.

When I was 13, I loved skateboarding. I would practice and practice and practice, doing tricks, sometimes hundreds of times a day, until I could get them right. Then, I would practice until I couldn't get them wrong. It brought me a lot of enjoyment and friendships, and it was a lot of fun. After a pretty major injury, I stopped skating when I was 16. At 20 years old, I decided I might enjoy picking the sport back up. After a few times at the skatepark, I quickly realized that while I remembered many of the tricks, I had lost the pinpoint balance that had come from riding daily for several years. It was a dangerous combination. I could do tricks that would have developed a lot of coordination and balance while learning them, without having the subsequent balance and coordination. I was falling off of ribs, half pipes, and handrails like it was nobody's business. It only took a few go-rounds at the skatepark to realize that persevering and being tenacious at redeveloping my balance was probably not something in my best interest. Sometimes, it's best to know when to quit. The old adage that winners never quit simply isn't true. Winners quit all of the time. They quit things that don't matter, they quit things that aren't getting them closer to the goal, they quit things that don't make a difference, and they quit things that aren't helping them.

> **WINNERS QUIT ALL OF THE TIME. THEY QUIT THINGS THAT DON'T MATTER, THEY QUIT THINGS THAT AREN'T GETTING THEM CLOSER TO THE GOAL, THEY QUIT THINGS THAT DON'T MAKE A DIFFERENCE, AND THEY QUIT THINGS THAT AREN'T HELPING THEM.**

Ultimately, being relentless is about being ruthless with yourself; relentlessly seeking out, dismantling, and destroying the things in our lives that keep us from being great. And relentlessly pursuing the disciplines, habits, and actions that make us great. Relentless isn't just about doing; sometimes, it's about being brave enough to stop doing, to admit we were wrong, and to course correct. It's about the ability to look in the mirror and say, "I was wrong," and then relentlessly attack the right direction. At the end of the day, relentless isn't something we do, it's *who we are*. Beware of the lollipop of mediocrity; one lick and you might suck for life.

CHAPTER 10

CONSISTENCY

con·sist·en·cy
/kənˈsistənsē/

noun

1. the achievement of a level of performance
that does not vary greatly in quality over time.[22]

C onsistency is the bridge between goals and achievements. Leaders do *consistently*, what others do sometimes. This is the key. Leaders are not doing something different than everyone else; they're doing the same things with more consistency. Leaders self-improve every day while the average person gets better sometimes.

> **LEADERS DO CONSISTENTLY,
> WHAT OTHERS DO SOMETIMES.**

Consistency allows the compounding of efforts to take place. It's a small win, stacked on top of a small win, on top of a small win, until the small wins become larger wins. Consistency creates compounding. When consistency is interrupted, the compounding halts. Imagine having invested money into the markets. As long as the money stays invested, it continues to compound. If the money is withdrawn, the compounding halts. It's the same with compounding efforts. Think about habit creation for a moment. The correct habits can make or break us. The formation of those habits is due to the repetition of a new thought or behavior, consistently, over time. Based on my personal opinion and experiences, it takes 21 -70 days to create a habit. The key here is those days need to happen consistently. If you stop for 2 days on day five, you don't start over on day 6; you start over on day one. This is precisely why so many have such a hard time creating the very habits they know will create success in their lives. Instead of recognizing inconsistency as the culprit, most people believe they are doing something wrong. This sets them on an endless quest for more information, when, in reality, we don't need more information, we need to act more consistently on the information we have.

Consistency in our actions is imperative, but as discussed in my previous book, *BYPRODUCT*, actions are actually the byproduct of our beliefs, and our beliefs are the byproduct of our thoughts. We must first create consistency in those two areas if we ever want to create consistency in our actions.

Have you ever met someone inconsistent in their thinking? One day, they are going to be a teacher, the next day, they are going to change the world with a new diet program, and the next day, they don't want to do anything but chill. Their inconsistency in thought and direction sends them bumping aimlessly through life. Their direction and destination are unpredictable, and they repel relationships, careers, and anything else that requires consistency and stability. They behave erratically and respond to different circumstances in a variety of unpredictable ways.

One of the greatest tools a leader can employ is developing behavioral and emotional consistency. Most people are emotional rollercoasters. There are plenty of those people out there. Few leaders can exhibit emotional steadfastness. It's a trait that attracts followers and leaders alike. In a world of constant inconsistency, people are drawn to stability with a powerful sort of magnetism. A leader's consistency breeds a safe and comfortable place for new leaders to grow, try, fail, and recalibrate. Inconsistency in leadership, or at home, creates an unstable environment. When you don't know if your leader is going to encourage you or tear you to shreds when you fail, you simply don't take the chance, you play it safe, and the team suffers. With emotionally consistent leaders, everybody knows what to expect, and that allows them some level of certainty in moving forward.

INCONSISTENCY OF BELIEF

Most of us are consistently inconsistent. Inconsistency of belief occurs when our underlying beliefs and thinking are not grounded in objective reality. With inconsistent belief comes all manner of duplicity. We want success, but our beliefs are clouded on the subject. Is it luck? Is it the right place, at the right time? Is it hard

MOST OF US ARE ONSISTENTLY INCONSISTENT.

work? Is it constant growth? With the inconsistency of belief, we take action in one direction for a while, but because we lack the clarity that action will produce, we seldom stay with it long enough to see results.

HABITS: THE AUTOPILOT OF LIFE

We don't choose our life, we choose our habits, and then, our habits choose our life. We, ultimately, are what we consistently do. Winners do all of the time, what losers do sometimes. According to the Massachusetts Institute of Technology, approximately 45 percent of everything we do on a daily basis is a result of habit. Leading so much of our life without our direct conscious control, one would be wise to look at and evaluate the quality of the habits they possess. Habits themselves are not good or bad, they simply are. They can be applied to any behavior or thought process. The byproduct of those habits are actions and subsequent outcomes. Whether

WE, ULTIMATELY, ARE WHAT WE CONSISTENTLY DO.

we are aware of it or not, we are all operating primarily off habit. Even people who would argue that they have trouble creating habits, really do have habits. They have the habit of inconsistency. Since habits are running our lives, it would make sense to identify and evaluate the habits we possess. We must evaluate the habits that create both good and bad outcomes. He who creates the habit of creating his habits will one day rule the world. Even if only their own world, that is still an impressive feat that very few will ever accomplish.

Have you ever noticed that the greats seem to dominate their field, almost effortlessly? Winners make it look easy because the process of winning has become habitual. Instead of requiring conscious energy and attention, the actions, mindsets, and effort expenditures happen autonomously.

One of the most unique things about habits is, when set up correctly, they automate many of the functions that previously consumed conscious effort. This frees up time and mental energy for the winner to create and develop even more positive and productive habits. Even though time is spent on executing the habits, zero time or mental energy is spent on the decision to use the habit or not. This provides great power to the people who selectively and purposefully develop habits. It quite literally gives them more time and mental bandwidth. The time others use to make decisions or to develop skill sets people with great habits have available. The greatest leaders create compounding habits. When a set of habits is established, the time, effort, and energy used in creating that habit are then used to create even more productive habits.

COMPOUNDED EFFORT: EFFORT IS NOT LINEAR

Compounded effort is very much like compounded interest. At first, growth is slow. It can look like not much is happening, but, over time, the compounding of effort and habits creates acceleration and exponential growth. Think about an investment that is removed from the market; it ceases to grow. It only begins growing again once it is reinvested. The same thing happens with compounding effort. When you miss a day, you don't just get to start over. As we just addressed, I believe it takes 21 days to build a habit. Many studies now conclude that it really takes an average of 59 to 70 days to form a habit.[23] In reality, I think it is both 21 days and 59 to 70 days. It takes 21 days to develop what I call an awareness-level habit. You have the formation of a new behavior or thought process, but it still requires conscious effort and energy to execute. Amateurs practice until they get it right; professionals practice until they can't get it wrong. Think about awareness habits as amateur habits. After 21 days, most people have amateur awareness-level habits. These habits are not subconsciously formed yet, and are repeatable and predictable, only as long as they are not interfered with. After 59 to 70 days, the habits are truly automatic. They require no conscious effort whatsoever and have now become part of who you are and what you do.

So, if it takes 70 days to create a habit, and you take a day off on day six, you don't just get a pick-up again at seven. You start over again, on day one, which is predominantly why most people don't have great habits. They never stay consistent enough to actually get through a 59 or 70 day uninterrupted habit creation. Period. When it comes to habit creation, consistency is everything. Anything done consistently, every day, for 59 or 70 days will become a habit, good or bad, purposefully or by default.

TRIGGER HABITS: A SNOWBALL CAN EVENTUALLY BECOME AN AVALANCHE

Habits beget more habits. The creation of certain habits actually facilitates the formation of other habits. These are often called trigger habits. They are the actions creating the pathway for multiple new habits. Think about people with addictive personalities. They create one addictive habit, and a litany of future addictive habits are likely to form. Statistically, people who smoke are also more likely to abuse alcohol and drugs and have any number of other habits that would generally be perceived as non-beneficial. In this case, smoking was the trigger habit, making it easier for all the other habits to follow. Whether directed positively or negatively, trigger habits affect our lives. For many, exercise is a trigger habit. If I'm exercising consistently in the morning, all of the other habits that move my day in a productive and positive direction, follow. Without the habit of physical fitness on a daily basis, my other habits struggle. Fitness is the trigger. It's the habit that makes the other habits effective and effortless. What are some of your trigger habits?

HABITS WORTH DEVELOPING

Since we are in control of the habits we possess or create, and simultaneously, have our lives dictated by them, it would make sense that we seek to instill great habits and eliminate negative ones.

I believe there are four areas of life that are "must win." Falling short in one of these areas actually negatively impacts every other area of life. The 4 Fs are the four areas that we need to get right. For me, my most impactful habits have always revolved around the four F's: Faith, Family, Fitness, and Finance. Stop and think about it for a second: "What good is it for someone to gain the whole world, yet forfeit their soul" (Mark 8:36, NIV). You could have finance and fitness and a great family, but without your faith, the joy ride is limited to your tenure on earth. Eternity can be an awfully long time to be on the wrong side of the deal. You might have a great family and great financial resources, in a wonderful spiritual life, but if your health is failing, you can't enjoy your family and your finances. The same is true for any combination of the 4 Fs. Without all four, a major negative pull on our lives begins. We've got to win in these four areas. Developing habits, purposefully, in these areas is what great leaders do. They don't leave it to chance, they leave it to change. In my War Room mentorship group at the VIP level, I provide them with a Key Performance Indicator, KPI, tracker. The KPI tracker helps leaders track the daily activities that will help them create wins in the 4 Fs of life. The tool allows them to see how consistently they act on those core fundamental activities daily. For some, it might be reading for 15 minutes a day, it could be walking a mile, it could be writing their spouse a note daily, or it could be making ten sales calls. Whatever it is, they've identified and tracked it on a daily basis until it becomes habitual. At that point, they can now set new targets and new actions they want to develop as habits and repeat the cycle.

15 MINUTES

Many people believe that habits are just too difficult to create or will take too much time. What I have found, in 15 years of leading people, is you can create massive life change with 15 minutes a day. We must, purposefully, create habits in the 4 F areas that allow us to live life fully. Here is an example of some of my habits. These may be different for you based on your goals in life.

Every single day, I start my day walking for 30 minutes, followed by a 2 mile run. I started that habit by walking for 15 minutes a day. Walking is an activity that virtually every able-bodied person can do, no matter how out of shape they are, and it is a trigger habit. I find that it gets me up and out of bed at the same time every day. It gets my blood pumping, calories burning, and it also allows me to piggyback on other things I need to get done like answering emails and texts. Since I am already up and walking, and it did not take any mental effort, I can direct time towards other productive things I won't have to do later in the day. Another habit is having a protein shake for breakfast every morning after my walk. This does a couple of things for me. Number one, it drastically reduces my calorie count for the meal by 500 to 700 calories a day. The other thing it does is save me time by not having to make food or go out somewhere. By changing this one habit, it saves me, on average, 15,000 calories a month and, approximately, 20 hours of deciding, traveling, and sitting in restaurants, etc. If you take the calorie count and time-savings and multiply it over months or years, that one habit saves me 50 pounds of excess weight and hundreds of hours a year. 15 minutes a day may not be enough to create mastery, but it is enough to create momentum. Start where you are, with what you have, and point yourself in the direction of your goals and dreams.

FAITH

One of the habits that I have developed around my faith is reading the Bible every evening before I go to bed. It takes me about five minutes to read one chapter a day. I spend another five minutes reflecting on what I read and applying it to my life. Sometimes, I write down lessons or ideas and use them later to create content. In literally 10 minutes a day, I make sure, every day, I spend time with God. The Bible app on my phone enables me to do this wherever I am, and many times, I don't wait until the end of the day to do so. If I've got a few minutes of downtime during my other daily activities, I'll jump on and read my chapter so I don't have to read it later. If you focus for just a few minutes every day on what God is teaching you and who He wants you to become, you will be amazed at how positive of a direction your life can move.

FAMILY

A habit I began in this area several years ago was sending an email to my wife every evening. Accused, as many men are, of being a poor communicator, what I found was, if every night I recap the day and talk about the events of the upcoming day, I would be initiating undistracted communication with the most important person in my life. Every single day, for over 8 years, I've been sending this email. Every day, in the morning, I get a reply email from Jess. Most days, we spend an enormous amount of time together. It's one of the benefits of being self-employed and a partner in business and in life. Whether we're launching a new product, starting a new venture, or maybe just relaxing around the house, there's never a day that goes by when we don't communicate the purposeful and meaningful things in our life.

FINANCE

There are a lot of little habits, financially, that can be put in place to help you excel. If you struggle financially, the other three Fs won't be nearly as rewarding. You'll always be bogged down with financial concerns, lack of resources, and inability to really live your best life in the other areas. One 5 minute habit that I developed was just paying attention to the markets; Real Estate markets, precious metals markets, the stock market, cryptocurrency, etc.

I look at these markets every day and try to skim through at least an article or two related to why they're moving in what ways. Over time, you begin to get an operating knowledge of investing and how markets work, as well as a basic business understanding. Another 15 minute habit that I developed was working daily on developing income producing skills. Find something you're good at and enjoy and people will pay you for it. Get really, really good at it, 15 minutes a day. In a year, you will have spent the equivalent of nearly 2.5 working weeks, solely focused on the improvement of the skill.

THREE OTHER POSITIVE HABITS TO DEVELOP

1. A GREAT MENTAL ATTITUDE

Developing the habit of keeping a great attitude, no matter what's going on around you, is one of the things that will set you apart in the world of leadership and success. When you control your inner state, no one can control you by manipulating your outer state. Anybody can be positive when things are going great, but it takes a real leader, and somebody with extreme mental toughness, to stay positive when things aren't going well. And that's when it counts most. It's when things are "hitting the fan" that we need positive, proactive leaders around. Our attitude is kind of like a default setting: It's positive, negative, or neutral. Most people will never raise their awareness enough to keep track of their attitude on a regular basis. Only the most self-aware leaders are able to accurately observe their own attitude and course-correct on their own.

Developing the habit of having a great attitude is a three-step process. The first step is awareness. We must be aware of our attitude on a consistent basis. The second step is exchanging poor attitudes for better attitudes, when they are recognized, and making a conscious decision to react in a positive manner, regardless of what's going on around you. What will help you make these exchanges permanent is repetition. You're not going to be great at this right out of the gate; you may not be great at this for days, or even weeks, and remember, a real habit can take between 59 and 70 days to create. Over time, you will see, in general, your attitude shift from negative to positive.

2. EMOTIONAL STATE

A second area, where it's imperative we develop habits, is around our emotional state. Emotional state differs from attitude in that attitude is an outlook or perspective that we filter our experiences through. Emotional state is more of a chemical reaction to our surroundings and circumstances. It's possible to have a great mental attitude and still not be controlling your emotional state. Think of the person who wins a big jackpot, and elated by his outcome, goes and gambles that jackpot and loses it. His attitude was great; he was on top of the world. The problem is, his emotional state caused him to make an irrational and incorrect choice. Most people are like roller coasters, emotionally. They're up, they're down, and they're upside down, all within the same 60 seconds.

PEOPLE WANT TO FOLLOW PEOPLE THAT ARE PREDICTABLE AND SAFE.

People want to follow people that are predictable and safe. Having control over your emotional state allows you to be predictable and safe, both for yourself and those around you. When somebody gets us angry, and we lose our temper, we also lose our control. Managing our emotional state is about staying in control, regardless of who or what is happening around us. It's about keeping our power and staying calm and collected, regardless of the environment we find ourselves in. Creating the habit of regulating our emotional state follows the same three-step process described above. We must first be aware of our emotional states and when we lose control of them. Second, we must exchange the current state for the desired state. Third, we must be patiently impatient as we go through a process of repetition to build that new habit of emotional control. Patient with the process and impatient with ourselves.

3. PERSONAL GROWTH

Make sure to invest in your future, because one day, you're gonna have to live in it. Self-development makes all of the difference in the world, yet it is easy to put off and neglect. The fact is, if we don't get better, things won't get better. We can not journey into a bright new future with our same old selves. Change is guaranteed, but growth is optional. Are you going to "grow through what you go through" or will you live the same year of your life 50 times and call it a life? Our ability

MAKE SURE TO INVEST IN YOUR FUTURE, BECAUSE ONE DAY, YOU'RE GONNA HAVE TO LIVE IN IT.

to grow our skill sets, our mindsets, and our thinking habitually and systematically will determine the altitudes to which we rise. Over time, the person that consistently gets better is going to win. You might be at the top of your game right now, but the game is changing, it's evolving, it's constantly reinventing itself. If you don't evolve with it, eventually, you'll become obsolete. One of the things I like to do is to read every single day; the two-minute cracks, the time between appointments, between meetings, or on the drive to work can be used to get better. One of the habits I formed early on was the habit of growing in the downtime. Getting yourself to pick up the

DON'T JUST EXIST, GROW

phone or push play on the audiobook, instead of mindlessly scrolling through social media, is going to make your fortune. It's going to grow your influence and help you become a better human being. Don't just exist, grow; don't just consume, produce. Get better!

CHAPTER 11

COMMITMENT

com·mit·ment
/kəˈmitmənt/

noun

1. the state or quality of being dedicated to a cause, activity, etc.

C ommitment is doing something, even when you no longer feel like it. It also appears to be one of the most misunderstood words in the world. All around us, a lack of commitment is evident, from soaring divorce rates, to massive delinquency in consumer debt, to the fact that we basically assume, most of the time, what most people say, they're not going to do. Commitment, in today's world, is more valuable than gold.

INTEREST VS COMMITMENT

When you're *interested* in something, you do it when it's convenient. When you're *committed* to something, you do it because you said you would. Commitment is the single greatest ingredient in execution. Staying with something long enough to see it through, regardless of changing

COMMITMENT IS THE SINGLE GREATEST INGREDIENT IN EXECUTION.

circumstances, adversities, and difficulties, will set you apart from the crowd, instantly. Everyone's committed, until it gets tough. Everyone's committed, until the circumstances change. Everyone's committed, until they just don't feel it anymore. Commitment isn't a feeling, it's a decision. It's a decision to do what you said, no matter what. To follow through on the promises you made to yourself, and to others, and to finish the job you started.

The world is full of starters. Starters are dime a dozen, but finishers are rare. Finishers are valuable. Finishers change the world. Commitment creates finishers. So much of success is hanging on longer than your competitor. It's sticking it out, and staying through. When everybody else is calling it quits, the committed are just getting started. So, let me ask you: Are you committed? Or, are you just interested? Because here's the hard truth: Interest isn't going to cut it. It's not enough to take you to the top of the game. It's not enough for you to build influence. it's not enough for you to leave a legacy. Those things require commitment and the courage to continue, no matter what. Do you have that courage? Are you a "whatever it takes, for as long as it takes" sort of person? Or, are you for sale?

NOT FOR SALE

What's it going to take to get you to give up on your big dreams and your big ambitions? A $10-an-hour pay raise? A negative family member? A health challenge? A troll on the internet?

IN EVERY INTERACTION, SOMEONE IS ALWAYS BUYING AND SOMEONE IS ALWAYS SELLING.

In every interaction, someone is always buying and someone is always selling. You've got to be sold, totally, completely, and fully sold on what you are doing. Until you're sold, you won't sell anybody else. And you've got to know that no matter what happens, no matter what comes against you, and no matter how hard it becomes, you're going to stay and finish the job.

Commitment builds trust. When you get in the habit of being known as somebody who does what you say you're going to do, you develop trust, making everything in life easier. Follow through. Become somebody who everyone can count on to get the job done. Imagine you are a child, and every morning, your father promises you ice cream at the ice cream shop after he arrives home from work. Every day, you can't wait for him to get home to take you for ice cream. But invariably, every day, something seems to come up. A phone call, a business meeting, an out-of-town friend. Day after day, week after week, month after month, every day, without fail, something comes up to interrupt the plans for ice cream. After a few months of this, you would eventually begin to believe that no matter

IF YOU DON'T TRUST YOURSELF, NOBODY ELSE WILL EITHER

what your dad says, you would not be going for ice cream. His words and his commitment do not mean much. Eventually, you would have eroded all trust in him and would likely end up despising him.

In the same way, we develop follow-through accounts with our friends, our family, coworkers, business partners, followers, and even ourselves. By delivering on and following through on commitments, we build the value of those accounts. With every single commitment made but not followed through on, we take a withdrawal from the account. The accounts of most people are negative in life, both personally and with others. When you commit to yourself but don't follow through, like the child in the story, you begin to distrust and eventually despise yourself. You simply don't trust yourself to finish the job. You don't trust yourself to follow through. You know, in your heart, you will not do what it takes. But here's a key: You must understand this—if you don't trust yourself, nobody else will either. The first step in building self-trust is keeping your promises, following through on what you said, and finishing the job. Commitment is what allows us to go to that place when it hurts and we want to give up, find that extra gear, throw it in overdrive, and finish the job.

Total commitment brings total freedom. Many people shy away from making tough commitments because they feel it will somehow limit them. They fear commitment may box them in and starve their options in the future. This couldn't be further from the truth. The most committed people I know are also the freest people I know. Total commitment brings total freedom. When you're truly committed, you

TOTAL COMMITMENT BRINGS TOTAL FREEDOM.

don't have to wonder anymore. You can stop running; you can stop searching and you can be at peace. Let me give an example. For those of you who are not married, a large amount of mental effort, time, energy, and money is spent pursuing romantic relationships. A lot of effort is put into investing in people, only to end up not being the one you're looking for. In fact, every day, in every way, your mind is spending at least some attention on looking for, evaluating, and cultivating relationships with people that potentially could be a romantic relationship option. Because you're not committed to one person, every person is an option. This leaves us in a constant state of permanent evaluation. In every interaction, we wonder, *What do they think about me?* or, *Do they feel the same as I do?* It consumes enormous amounts of time, effort, and energy.

For those of you who are married, the search has stopped. You no longer go into the world with this constant evaluation. The time, effort, emotion, and energy you used to put into finding her or him is no longer required. You don't have to wonder where you stand or where they stand. You've made a commitment to each other. In that commitment is total freedom; freedom from all of the running and all the searching and all the façades. The same is true as it relates to our goals, dreams, and life calling. When we're truly committed, we don't have to search anymore. We can say no to the good things that take us away from the great things. We can have peace, knowing who we are, where we are, and where we're going. Total commitment is the only thing that can bring peace; knowing you've planted your flag; here you stand, and here you will fight. Total commitment gives you that extra little edge that sets you apart from the competition.

A LITTLE BIT MORE!

"It's never crowded along the extra mile."[24]

Get in the habit of over-delivering. It's one of the most profitable habits to have. Whether it's in the area of faith, fitness, family, or finances, doing more than you committed to will result in incredible trust and open doors, wherever you go in life. Just this morning, as I finished up my run, I was challenged internally to go just a little bit further, to run past the finish line, to give it just a little bit more. All progress is a growth of some form. It's doing something that hasn't been done before; it's going faster or pushing further. It's been said that how we do the little things is how we do everything. Getting in the habit of doing just a little bit more than expected, just a little bit more than promised, just a little bit more than you committed to, is the cornerstone of commitment. Anyone can promise, but few deliver. And it's a rare few that over-deliver.

"There's a man in the world who is never turned down, whatever he chances to stray;

GET IN THE HABIT OF OVER-DELIVERING.

he gets the glad hand in the populous town, or out where the farmers makes hay; he's greeted with pleasure on deserts of sand, and deep in the aisles of the woods; wherever he goes there's a welcoming hand-he's the man who delivers the goods." -Walt Whitman[25]

In his book *The Outliers,* Malcolm Gladwell talks about the 10,000-hour rule.[26] The concept basically purports it takes about 10,000 hours to become an expert at anything. Greatness pays, mediocrity does not. Most people are, by definition, most people. They're average. They could be great, but they fail to put in the time required to develop greatness. Instead, they invest a few hundred or a few thousand hours, get disappointed, distracted, or discouraged, and then move on to a different venture, where, again, they begin at zero. Five career changes later, they've invested well over 10,000 hours, but not in the same direction, and have mastery of nothing. Commitment is sticking through it until you are a master until you're truly great and at the top of your game. Most people stop partway through and start over at something new. Here's a key: If you want to stop starting over in life, stop quitting, and get committed.

DISCIPLINE: THE WATCHWORD OF SUCCESS

Discipline is the backbone of commitment. It's one of those words everyone wishes wasn't in this book. It's one of those unfortunate realities. But here's the truth: We all have discipline in our lives: we either have self-discipline or are disciplined by others. Every high achiever knows nothing great, and nothing lasting will ever be accomplished without ample amounts of discipline. Discipline is the ability to show up every day, no matter what's happening in your life, and bring your A game. It is the bridge between goals and accomplishment. It's the watchword of high achievers. It's also one of the most misunderstood words in this book. Whether we realize it or not, we all have discipline. The question is, will it be internal discipline that pushes us out of our comfort zone into growth, or will it be the external discipline, provided by a boss, a quota, or a deadline, that forces us to act? Those who aren't self-disciplined will eventually be disciplined by others.

Discipline, really self-discipline, is the one thing setting you apart from all the talkers and great idealists. The ability to bring something through to fruition and execute is what allows you to transform those words into results.

Those who lack discipline are constantly in emergency mode, scrambling frantically to meet the deadline and complete the task. But, when you stay prepared, you don't have *to get* prepared.

In any endeavor, the newness and excitement of the beginning provide us with momentum and energy. In the same way, the sense of the finish line and accomplishment help to pull us the final inches to completion. But, it's in the middle that most dreams die. They die, because the only pathway through the middle, once the excitement from the beginning has worn off and the finish line is not yet in sight, is the discipline to act in the right direction. It's the power to get through the middle.

THE TWO KINDS OF DISCIPLINE

Most people dislike discipline because they associate the word with the first of two kinds of discipline.

CONSCIOUS DISCIPLINE

This is where you consciously exert effort and control over yourself. Your behavior, and your will to do something you otherwise wouldn't naturally do, require attention and commitment. Conscious discipline will almost always be required to start and move through new projects. In my book, *Byproduct*, I discuss the idea that actions are the byproducts of beliefs and happen quite naturally. Conscious discipline is a forced action without the belief needed to automate it. It takes effort, energy, and constant vigilance. It can often seem unpleasant, and by definition, it is not something we would have chosen to do naturally. These are tasks or activities we know we need to do to accomplish the goal, but we have not automated them yet as habits, so we must choose them continuously.

UNCONSCIOUS DISCIPLINE

The second sort of discipline is unconscious discipline. This is where the act or behavior still happens, but it doesn't require constant energy and attention to maintain. This is a pro athlete that hits the gym 3 hours per day, 6 days a week. At some point, the athletes' conscious discipline filled in with their underlying belief system, move to an unconscious activity. It is now just something the athlete does. It's part of their routine and doesn't need to be managed.

This is the person who rises at 4:30 a.m. and has accomplished more by the time most people wake up than others do all day. At first, the discipline is hard, it's conscious, but

SMALL CONSISTENT EFFORTS IN THE SAME DIRECTION, OVER TIME, CREATE MASSIVE RESULTS.

over time, it becomes autonomous, and no longer requires effort. In fact, that person's operating system becomes so autonomous, this person may actually find it hard to sleep in when they can. Their body is literally wired to wake up at 4:30 a.m., even if they don't need to.

One of the major hidden keys to massive success is found in transforming our required discipline from a conscious effort to easy automatic action. This happens when we create alignment between our thinking and beliefs. When asked by a reporter about his parent's involvement in his hockey success, Wayne Gretzky responded, "Nobody had to make me shoot pucks for 4 hours a day, my parents didn't make me stay home from the movies with my friends to practice, I wanted to do it. I wanted to shoot pucks more than anything."

That is the perfect illustration of total alignment between thinking and belief. Many little boys grow up wanting to be NHL stars. They understand the need to shoot pucks and work on stickhandling and skating. But why did Wayne Gretzky do it for four hours a day, when other boys might've only done it for a few hours a week? The answer, Wayne Gretzky believed his diligence and discipline would pay off. Despite knowing that practice would improve them, only one player did it. Nothing great is ever accomplished without incredible levels of discipline pulling us beyond the ranks of the average and ordinary.

Everything worth doing, becoming, or having will require us to leave the comfortable and familiar, and institute disciplines we simply do not possess right now. Discipline is what allows us to take large tasks and accomplish them in manageable parts. Small consistent efforts in the same direction, over time, create massive results. Most people are looking for the big break, the big relationship, the big opportunity, but winning big rarely comes from these larger-than-life moments. Winning big is the culmination of small things, done consistently, over time, which is exactly why most people don't win. They think there must be a different way, something more, something different, something big and magical. They are so busy looking and preparing for the big break, they forget to do the seemingly insignificant things along the way.

YOU CAN'T CRAM FOR LIFE

One of the most pervasive, yet easy-to-recognize mindsets, which illustrates this "overlooking" of the small disciplines in favor of larger more aggressive action, is the cram. College students have the propensity to cram for hours and hours, before a final exam, instead of just reading and completing the assignments as they come in small bites. Most people put off the daily manageable disciplines and end up playing catch-up, consuming large amounts of their time, effort, and mental energy trying to learn quickly what should've been learned periodically. We see the same sort of cramming mindset in virtually every area of life. People experience a health scare and, all of a sudden, a large amount of time, effort, and energy is spent trying to get back to health, instead of investing small amounts of energy on a daily basis to maintain great health. You see, marriage and children could be largely ignored for long periods of time, only to stop the world in its tracks when they are about to come crashing down. Instead of managing those marriage and family dynamics on a daily basis, they now require a complete and total interruption of every other area of life in order to keep them on track.

We should desire to be known as people of great discipline. Discipline is like the steel support beams of a skyscraper, the higher you build the building, the stronger those beams need to be. When our disciplines are strong, they can support the weight of a life well-lived.

CHAPTER 12

FOCUS

fo·cus
/ˈfōkəs/

noun

1. the center of interest or activity.

I magine a laser beam begins cutting through the metal core of a vault. Sparks are flying everywhere, and the black steel of the vault turns into bright orange molten metal right before your eyes. What is the difference between a flashlight and a laser beam? In a word, focus.

That is the power of light when it's focused. Now, imagine the faint yellow glow of the parking lot lights in a late-night game of pick-up basketball. What's the similarity between the two? Both the laser and the parking lights are forms of light. What is *dissimilar* between them is the level of focus applied to the light. While the laser beam is ultrafocused and incredibly powerful, the parking lot light takes the same energy source and disperses it over a much larger and less focused area. As it is with light, our ability to focus our energies, and direct them, consistently and continuously, toward the same end, creates a laserlike power in our lives. That focus allows us to cut through any and all obstacles in our path. Yet similarly, when our energies are unfocused and undirected, we can expend them without significantly brightening the world. Great lives are the byproduct of great focus.

FOCUS IS FINITE

We only have so much available brain space, time, emotional effort, and energy. They are all finite. Think of it as a pie.

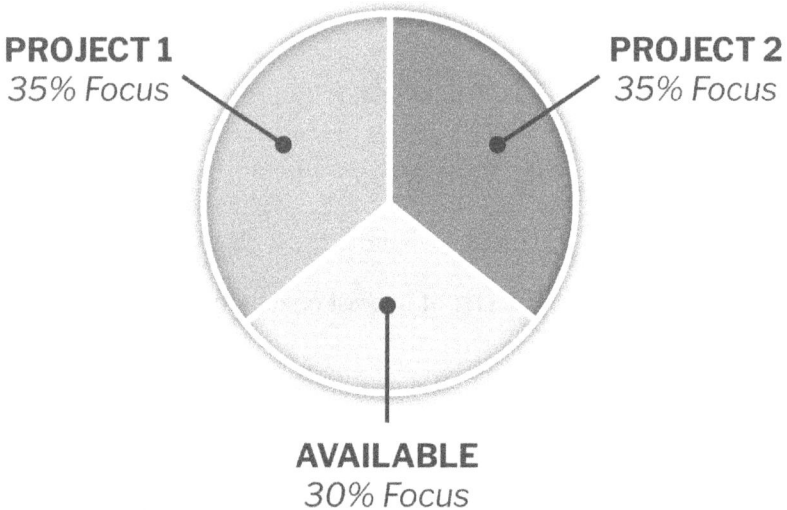

PROJECT 1
35% Focus

PROJECT 2
35% Focus

AVAILABLE
30% Focus

We have a finite amount of focus available. Let's imagine that a project requires 35% of the total available focus in order to reach completion. What you will find is everything in life requires a certain critical mass of focus and energy to complete. Without applying that threshold level of focus, the project simply doesn't finish. Take, for instance, two projects both requiring about 35% of the available focus. Both have the capacity for completion because the required focus allotment is below the 100% that is available. After completion, there is still energy and focus available for something else.

Now, let's imagine that same scenario but instead of two projects, there are five. If the available focus was split evenly between the five tasks at 20% each, none of the tasks would be completed. Why? Because our focus is finite. When we focus on too much, we complete too little. One of the greatest tools of success is the power of saying no. The more we say yes, the less effective we become. We only have so much ability to focus. Once that ability is watered down below the completion threshold, we start dropping the ball. You can be successful at anything you want, but you can't be successful at everything you want, at least not at the same time. One of the keys that unlock massive success in the lives of elite performers is the ability to say no to the good so there is room for the great. They are laser beams focused on the few critical

> YOU CAN BE SUCCESSFUL AT ANYTHING YOU WANT, BUT YOU CAN'T BE SUCCESSFUL AT EVERYTHING YOU WANT, AT LEAST NOT AT THE SAME TIME.

issues, while the rest of the population shines their parking lot light on anything and everything that comes their way. The focus-challenged person becomes "the Jack of all trades" and the master of none.

BUSY AS A BADGE OF HONOR

So many people today wear the label busy as a badge of honor. "How's life?" someone asks. "Busy," they reply. "I'm so busy." Busy this, busy that, and really, for the most part, they are busy … just busy going nowhere. There is a difference between busy and productive. Pros systematically eradicate busyness and over-commitment from their lives. Early in the journey, we tend to measure our successes by our yeses, but as we mature, we realize yes isn't always best. In fact, it takes a lot of no to

> THERE IS A DIFFERENCE BETWEEN BUSY AND PRODUCTIVE.

many good things to create the focus required to win at the truly important things. Most people's lives are so full of nonsense, they have no room left to win when greatness finds them.

FOCUS ON A FEW THINGS

Thinking again about the finite focus pie graph, it's important we become intentional about where our time and attention are placed. We need to pick one, or at most, two major areas to focus on at the same time. We simply don't have the brain power to focus on scaling the business, having a great family life, maintaining our fitness, hitting the guy's night twice a week, coaching our kid's little league team, and singing in the choir at church, all at the same time. We may attempt to accomplish all of those things simultaneously, but they will be done average at best, if at all. The greats pick one or two areas and drive towards mastery or unconscious competence at those few things. Once that level of mastery is reached, by definition, it no longer requires brain power to maintain competence; it has become habitual. Only once a habit has been formed can we divert our focus to developing other areas of life.

One of the most alluring schemes of the enemy is to crush your focus by creating an abundance of good things on which to spend your time and energy. It's not even bad things that the enemy uses. Sometimes, he uses good things that divert your attention from the great things, keeping you stuck in the same place.

To make serious, substantial progress, we need to identify the one or two most pressing areas of life and stop participating in everything else.

"Well Ian, you don't understand, I couldn't do that … what about … but they need me … but …."

Cut the crap. We always do what we ultimately want to do. It's easier to hide under the cover of chronically overbooking than to face the fact that we aren't making quality choices about where to spend our time and effort. That's true discipline. It's not saying no to things you know are bad, it's saying no to things you know are good but keep you from being great. Start with the end in mind, and focus on the things that will get you there.

TO-DON'T LIST—LESS IS MORE

The best yeses often come through strategic nos. Just because something is good, doesn't mean it's good for you. Here's another truth, just because something feels right doesn't make it right. Feelings are liars. It's rarely negative things keeping us from our destiny but rather positive things that have been misprioritized. The best question to ask yourself when deciding between a plethora of positive options is, "Is this getting me closer to or further from my dream?" If the answer is further from, stop doing it, now. If the answer is yes, keep doing it, or start doing it, but evaluate often to measure effectiveness.

Yes, a horse and buggy will get you from NYC to LA. But so will a car, a train, and a plane. All much faster and more efficient than the buggy. One of the greatest tools I've seen deployed consistently in the lives of super achievers is the use of the "to-don't list." Most of us are familiar with the to-do list, the seemingly endless train of tasks ahead of us to complete and check off. Most of us function well off a to-do list. It helps us to stay focused and prioritize our lives. The to-don't list is the opposite. It's a list of things to eliminate from our plates. Most things that most people do on a daily basis really don't need to be done at all, or at least not by us. So, how do we know the difference between what must be done, what must be done by us, and what could be done by others or not at all? The Eisenhower Matrix[27] provides us with a great framework for understanding where our time and effort should be going and, just as importantly, where it shouldn't be going.

THE EISENHOWER MATRIX

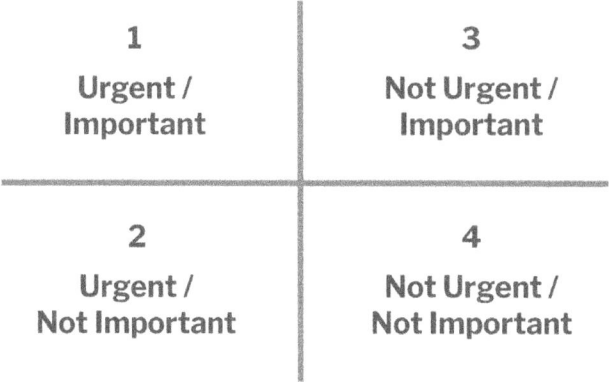

1 Urgent / Important	3 Not Urgent / Important
2 Urgent / Not Important	4 Not Urgent / Not Important

DO

There are two quadrants in the Eisenhower Matrix that house tasks that have to be done by us. They can't be outsourced, they can't be neglected, and there is no escaping them. The first of those quadrants is urgent and important. These are the things that are necessary to be done by us and have a lasting effect on the quality of our life. This could be something like your kids' birthday party; it's not something you can delegate. It's also something you can't miss without great consequences later in life. Children remember milestones and markers in their life forever. It's got to be done, and it's got to be done by you. Get clear and get committed to doing the things in this part of this matrix. Here, you must deliver. These are the areas you can't afford to mess up.

The other quadrant that can't be outsourced is important but not urgent. These are the things that really do move the needle in our lives but do not have a timeline attached to them. Like the urgent and important, they can't be done by anybody else. No one else is responsible for our self-improvement, for the quality of our health, for what we put into our relationships, or for growth and discipline; that's on us. Furthermore, nobody forces us to do those things, which is why so many people don't do them or don't do them consistently.

DELEGATE: URGENT BUT NOT IMPORTANT

In this quadrant of the Eisenhower Matrix, you find life-sucking tasks. Doing the dishes, mowing the lawn, cleaning the house, getting gas, or washing the car. It is necessary to take care of these things. They, ultimately, can't be put off. They present themselves with urgency, but the key is this, they don't necessarily need to be done by you. You can't let these things go forever, but you can delegate them to others to do. Whether you clean the house or a house cleaner cleans the house, the house is clean. It is largely irrelevant how the house got cleaned, only that it happened. There are many people who feel overwhelmed in life, trapped at their current level of achievement because they refuse to let go of these insignificant matters. You do not become less valuable when you don't do these things; it's actually quite the opposite. You become more valuable by *not* doing them. When you delegate, you have more time, effort, and energy to focus on the things that move the ball downfield.

DUMP

Wasting time is the favorite pastime of the average and ordinary. Many of us spend an inordinate amount of time on areas in our life that are neither important nor urgent. These activities just don't make a difference in the overall accomplishments of our life. Yet, amidst their relative uselessness, we choose to do them anyway. Things like the overconsumption of entertainment, playing video games, and hanging out with people that aren't going anywhere in life can be some of the largest resource grabs. Time spent here offers no return, and time, once wasted, is gone forever. What I have found in 15-plus years of coaching top achievers is that most people can create super high levels of success in their life simply by eliminating time spent in this quadrant and redirecting that time to the more important areas of life.

THE ONE THING

In his book *The One Thing*[28], Gary Keller presents the idea that at any time, there is ONE thing we can be doing that is more important than all other things we have to do. And when that one thing is complete, it makes everything else easier or unnecessary. The one thing is really about focus. Specifically, focus on the most important thing. Many of us are professionals at focusing on all the wrong things. When we focus on and accomplish the most important things in our lives, we are sure to be moving in the right

MOST PEOPLE MAJOR IN THE MINORS.

direction. Most people major in the minors. We spend all sorts of time, effort, and energy focusing on completing unimportant tasks, leaving us with little time or energy for the really important ones.

In life, there are many good things. But, as researcher, author, speaker, and consultant Jim C. Collins says, "Good is the enemy of great."[29] It's fine to play ping-pong; you might actually get a bit of exercise and improve your hand-eye coordination, but unless you're Forrest Gump, being a success at ping-pong isn't going to make other areas of your life easier. Will it improve your marriage or your relationship with your kids? Probably not. It probably won't increase your net worth, give you more influence, or help you change the world. It's a fine thing; it's just not the main thing.

> **IT'S EASIER TO START SOMETHING NEW THAN DISCIPLINE YOURSELF TO FINISH SOMETHING OLD.**

Some things are indeed great and aid in accomplishing many other things. For example, when we focus on building a residual recurring income, it gives you more time to spend with your spouse and kids. Also, you may not have the financial stress most people carry. Additionally, it rolls over into the area of health as we eat better, have access to better medical care, and achieve more physically. It allows you to be more generous with both your time and money. That's a pretty powerful ability.

We must learn to ask ourselves this question as we search for the one thing to prioritize in our life: Is doing this making other things in my life easier or harder? Focus on priorities in that order. We start with the most impactful one-thing ideas and move down the list until all are complete. As we battle to gain clarity and focus in our lives, I believe, there is value in discussing the opposite of focus, *distraction.*

Distracted is what you get when you forget where you're going. Like a moth to the light, most people will quickly abandon whatever it was they were working towards to approach what is new and exciting. It's easier to start something new than discipline yourself to finish something old. It's the shiny object syndrome, and it's created by choice overload. Too many options and too many possibilities lead many into a place of analysis paralysis. Like the person who scrolls through 200 movies on Netflix and decides to watch nothing, when we succumb to option overload, we move away from significance and into surrender.

We are often tempted to move from our current situation, where growth is hard fought and every inch is a mile, to a new situation where growth and achievement are easier. If you've ever been on an exercise regimen for any length of time, you know that the gains and weight loss come relatively easily. For the first several months, or even a year or two, progress comes quickly, but once you shed the excess pounds or develop the underdeveloped muscle groups, the gains become a harder fight and less noticeable. Professional bodybuilders will spend 4 to 6 hours a day in the gym to make, sometimes, unnoticeable improvements to the naked eye. This is known as the law of diminishing returns. The rate of gain slows down, and the cost to achieve it increases.[30] It's at this point, most people jettison their current path and look for easier gains in new ventures. It is precisely why so few people focus long enough on any given thing to master it. The gains come easier in the beginning and get progressively harder as we go. A novice piano player may take some classes and practice for an hour a day, and in a year, their skill set has grown by a thousand percent. Check in with that same novice ten years later as a master, and she may have only improved one-tenth of one percent in the last year, even practicing eight hours a day. The better we get, the harder we must push ourselves for smaller and smaller gains. When this law hits in real life, it's like running into a brick wall. Predictable and easy progress is now a struggle. The fun turns to work, and at this point, even the coolest and most rewarding careers and hobbies many people abandon. To stop grinding for inches, and pursue a new, more enjoyable endeavor with easy gains again, becomes alluring.

Sometimes, we're distracted by other opportunities, other things we think we might enjoy or take an interest in. But many times, distractions come in the form of life, family issues, health challenges, drama, problems with coworkers, competition, and regulation. All forms of distraction. Pros learn how to win anyway.

DISTRACTIONS EQUAL DESTRUCTION

Most of us are not held from our goals by obstacles but rather by clearer paths to lesser goals. The enemy doesn't need to destroy us if he can distract us. It is then, distracted, we destroy ourselves.

THE ENEMY DOESN'T NEED TO DESTROY US IF HE CAN DISTRACT US.

Distractions interrupt focus and kill productivity. They come in several forms. Here, we will discuss the three main universes of distraction.

1. The Pleasantly Unpleasant—These are largely self-imposed distractions that bring us some sort of pleasure, relief, or enjoyment. In other words, these are distractions we choose. It may be entertainment, television, sporting events, alcohol, etc. These things are not inherently bad. They become negative when they interrupt or limit your ability to put in the time, effort, and focus required to attain your goals. Most people would rather cheer for millionaires on TV than do the work to become one themselves. These distractions need to be identified and eliminated. By avoiding these unnecessary distractions, most people could accomplish incredible things.

2. Attention Dominators—These are distractions that vie for our time and attention but hold very little weight in the ultimate outcome of our lives. Think housework, mowing the lawn, taking out the trash, getting the car washed, running errands, grocery shopping, gossip, people problems, attention seekers, etc. These are all things that have to be dealt with but are not life-altering. These distractions should be identified and delegated away from you. Although they require completion, you're not the one to complete them. Get these tasks off your list, and these people to a counselor.

3. Needy People—"Poor planning on your part does not necessitate an emergency on mine."[31]

The world is full of people who need you to solve their problems, NOW! Almost always, those problems are created by their own lack of execution. We could spend our whole lives responding to the emergencies of others. When we are constantly reacting to others, we may never accomplish the purpose and destiny assigned to our lives. I'm not saying we don't help people, but think of it in the famous airplane oxygen mask analogy: Before helping others, make sure to secure your own mask. The best way to help others is to rise above the level of distraction and delay and lack that plagued them.

FOCUS THROUGH CHUNKING

One of the great keys to creating and sustaining focus is chunking. Chunking is the practice of taking large and drawn-out goals and breaking them into shorter and more attainable pieces. Measurable milestones that lead you to your desired outcomes need to be identified, targeted, and then celebrated when achieved. The moving of a giant mountain begins with the first stone. It can be hard to stay excited about a goal that seems too far off. One of a leader's primary objectives when cultivating a culture of focus is breaking down the vision into the visible, something the team, the client, and the customer can see, identify with, and internalize. The leader needs to be able to see the entire vision and the 30,000-foot view of the situation the follower does not. Grandiose visions are often demoralizing, and even more often, left incomplete because the path to attaining them is vague. Chunking allows everyone to clearly see the next step on the path. The leader, in many ways, is like a GPS. They need to know the destination and the direction to best chart the path. The follower, on the other hand, simply needs to know the next turn in the path or process. That is why chunking is so critical. It allows our teams to have simple, easy, and direct steps to take to execute the vision. Almost anyone can do almost anything for short periods of time with clearly constructed goals, milestones, and rewards.

URGENCY

Part of focus is urgency. What can be done, should be done, and should be done now.

Winners do today what everybody else put off until tomorrow. Urgency is the opposite of procrastination, where work expands to the longest possible time to completion. Urgency is where timeframes are collapsed and results explode. Do today what others won't do; you can have tomorrow what others don't. We all have the exact same amount of time in a day, you, me, the president, it's exactly the same. What makes heroes out of some men and nobody out of others is how they choose to use it. Empires are literally built in the time other people waste.

Urgency is about now. It's about doing the most productive thing possible at any given moment. It's about playing like there is someone chasing you trying to take everything you have worked for away. It's living like today is the very last day of your life, getting in every ounce of value from every available minute. Great leaders understand the importance of being able to operate under urgency. They also understand the importance of their ability to create organizational urgency. Urgency instills focus because it puts deadlines on our deliverables. When we're playing against the clock, we don't have the luxury of distraction.

"Necessity is the mother of all invention"[32] and urgency is one of the major components of necessity. Urgency forces us to not just find a solution but to find it *now*. When we finish now, later is available for new and greater endeavors. When we finish later, later is used to finish what should've been done now.

WHAT DOES URGENCY LOOK LIKE?

It looks like a relentless hustle all of the time. Great teams and great leaders create urgency, even when there isn't any. They know it will force them to get the most out of themselves and their teams. Imagine running late to the start of our favorite sports team kickoff. You become the definition of urgent, weaving in and out of traffic, looking at speed limits as more like general suggestions, and walking so fast you look like a professional speed walker. We are urgent for the game, yet we don't operate most days with that same level of urgency for the things that really matter in life. When we get urgent about the important things in our life, we create more time, more peace, and more results. Here is an urgency checkup for some of the most important areas of our lives.

GET URGENT ABOUT YOUR HEALTH

When we get urgent about our health, we will not only experience a longer life but a better quality of life along the way. We have more energy, more focus, and more years with which to invest our energy and make a difference. Don't start the diet tomorrow, start it today. Don't go to the gym tomorrow, go to the gym right now. It's easy to delay the sense of urgency with our health because the cause-and-effect reaction is delayed. When we eat the double cheeseburger, we don't instantly gain 25 pounds or have a heart attack. When we put off going to the gym, we don't instantly lose our flexibility, strength, and energy. But over time, all of those things add up. We've got to be vigilant about making health an urgent priority in our life.

GET URGENT ABOUT FAMILY

What value is it to win in business and lose your family along the way? No one sets out with the goal of destroying their marriage, damaging their kids, and creating havoc in the family. They simply aren't focused on not doing those things. Your family spells love t.i.m.e. We must make it a priority to schedule time and attention with those who are most important to us. The hard part is, nobody is demanding that we do it. There is no performance review, no deadline vying for our attention, and as we hustle for the more urgent but less important, our families take a well-intentioned seat on the back burner.

GET URGENT ABOUT SPIRITUAL LIFE

Virtually every decision we make, interaction we have, and value system we hold is driven, or at least in some way, shaped by our spiritual development. When we know who we are and whose we are, it shapes our belief system and worldview. This subsequently creates our actions and inactions. It's not possible to achieve fulfilling and meaningful victories while being spiritually void. Many high achievers accomplish incredible heights and find the imagined fulfillment of the victory to be a mirage. They often ask, "Is that all there is?" You are not your accomplishments, your net worth, or your academy awards. One day, those will all be gone. When we put our identity into achievements and accolades, we will spend our lives chasing, pursuing, and striving. When we root out identity in God, we can spend our life living, growing, and serving. When we live life like that, all of the accolades chase us. You are God's child, loved and paid for with a price. No matter what you've done, no matter how far away you think you are, you're not too far. The truth is, most of us compartmentalize God. He's a lucky rabbit's foot in our back pocket when we're in a bind or we need something to go our way. When our spiritual well-being is urgently attended to instead of dusted off when needed most, the other things in life take care of themselves. When you are spiritually strong at the core, it helps you to win in the other areas of your life.

GET URGENT ABOUT CASH FLOW

If you take care of money, one day, money will take care of you. As much as the current power structures would like to keep you resenting money, despising money, and being wholly uneducated about money, money is a tool with which we navigate this life. Much like a car is a tool to help us navigate the roads, money is a tool to help us navigate life. The more of it we have, the more options we have. We have more and better options when it comes to our healthcare, our food choices, schooling for our children, crime rates around our homes, and opportunities for the future, to name just a few. There is a war on wealth today in the United States. The government and school systems vilify those with money because they know that wealth creates independence. When you are in control of your own wealth, you are not dependent on the government or your employer for your well-being. Power hates independence because independence is the one thing that jeopardizes the controlling interests' future. What's your boss going to think when you tell them no to their demands because you don't need the money?

Money, like people, won't go where it's not desperately wanted, and it won't stay until it finds a home that respects it and values it. We have got to be urgent about becoming financially independent. Financial independence can be measured as the amount of time you could go sustaining your current standard of living without having to work to generate an income. We need to become urgent about maximizing our income and savings, creating residual income, and minimizing expenses. Until we are financially free, we are not really free at all.

GET URGENT ABOUT YOUR DREAMS

Dreams have a shelf life, and if you don't act now, you probably never will. Tomorrow is the mythical land where 99 percent of all human achievement is stored. Take action. Do something, anything, to move yourself in the direction of your dream today. It's not that what we want is too hard, it's that what we settle for comes too easy. As time passes, our vision, passion, and fire for our goals and

DREAMS HAVE A SHELF LIFE

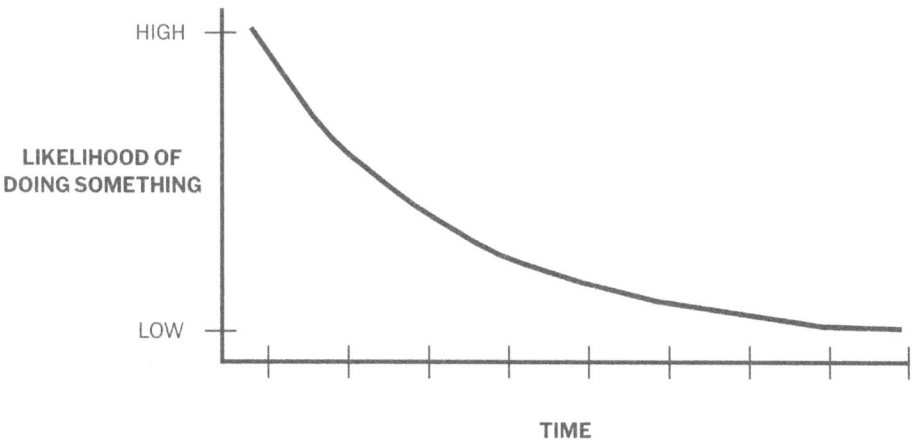

dreams slowly erode. The sands of time wear them down with each passing day. It's Newton's Law: "An object at rest remains at rest … unless acted on by an unbalanced force." You are that force, and you have to act on your life because nobody else will.

LIKELIHOOD OF DOING SOMETHING

HIGH

LOW

TIME

CREATING URGENCY

Urgency is a function of belief. It's really a fear of loss reaction. When we understand this about urgency, we can help create it by visualizing the potential losses incurred by our inaction. The girl, the business, the respect, the promotion. What will you lose by not acting? When we believe we are in danger, or that if we don't act now we will miss the opportunity of a lifetime, we are compelled into action. Action is always a byproduct of belief. If we aren't acting urgently, it's because we don't believe we need to.

A trait of all great leaders is their ability to get urgent about important things; to do today what others put off until tomorrow or next week or never. But it's not enough to just be urgent, we must be urgent about the right things.

There are many people who have a great deal of urgency towards trivial things. They don't move the needle and never will, yet people move heaven and earth to attend to them. Recall the Eisenhower Matrix from earlier in the book. In this matrix, all tasks or actions are split into 4 categories. Those categories are as follows:

URGENT AND IMPORTANT

URGENT AND UNIMPORTANT

NON URGENT AND IMPORTANT

NON URGENT AND UNIMPORTANT

Most success is locked inside what people do with the important but not urgent quadrant. These are things like investing in your marriage, self-development, health, and quality time with your kids. They are unbelievably important but at the same time, no one is holding a gun to your head to make you do those things. If we aren't careful they get done last or sometimes not at all. Champions in life learn to create urgency around the important but non urgent areas of life. There are many ways that leaders create this urgency, and here we will discuss a few.

1. CLARITY AND DEFINITENESS OF PURPOSE.

When you don't know where you are going, any path will do.

The more clear we are on what we want and why it's important to us, the more emotionally engaged we can become. When we're clear on what we want, we become clear on what we don't want. With the end in mind, we can reverse engineer the path to get it.

The component pieces of a desired outcome are called inputs. In other words, these are the pieces we put

WHEN YOU DON'T KNOW WHERE YOU ARE GOING, ANY PATH WILL DO.

together to achieve our desired goal. The stronger the link we can create between input actions and desired outcomes, the more we will believe those actions to be important. The stronger our beliefs, the more potent and consistent our actions in attaining them will be. The more engaged we are in the attainment of what we want, the more serious we become about the steps to possess that outcome. Clarity, engagement, and the connection between input and outcome create an autonomous sense of urgency. Many people are destined to wander and bump through life because they are unclear of what they want and why they want it. When what we want is unclear or unemotional, the steps to get there don't hold much value to us. We understand them at a thinking level to be good things but don't believe them to be necessary for our lives. Get clear about what you want, why you want it, and what steps will create that outcome.

WHEN WE'RE CLEAR ON WHAT WE WANT, WE BECOME CLEAR ON WHAT WE DON'T WANT.

Spend just one minute every day visualizing that outcome and emotionally connecting to it to create massive urgency in your life.

2. DEADLINES AND LIMITS

Set deadlines, even when they aren't real. Very few times in nature has there ever been witnessed more productivity than in observing the American employee preparing to leave for vacation. It's funny but it's true: when deadlines loom, productivity soars. Work expands into the time allotted for it. Great leaders understand that creating faux finish lines can instill a great sense of urgency and foster ingenuity. Buffered deadlines are one of the keys super achievers use to create urgency and execution. A buffered deadline is an artificially created time limit that is reasonably in front of the actual drop dead date. Think about the last time you took a final exam in high school or maybe college. When did you begin studying for that exam aggressively? If you're like most people, you started studying the night before. When we get our teams to compete to hit deadlines that are actually well in advance of the real delivery date, we ensure our ability to consistently deliver results. Most people and businesses play at a level where the stars have to align in perfect order for on-time execution to occur. We need to play the game of life at a high enough level where we can take a couple of bad calls from the refs and still win the game. Buffered deadlines allow teams to stay far enough ahead that they can adjust for unforeseen interruptions, circumstances, and challenges.

WORK EXPANDS INTO THE TIME ALLOTTED FOR IT.

Many who are in the habit of failing are also prone to running right up to project deadlines. They don't anticipate problems or hiccups, and when they arise it's usually too late and deadlines are missed. Leaders anticipate problems and issues and understand that an overabundance of time and resources actually dulls creativity and urgency. Many times it's not what we lack that holds us back but rather what we have that others don't. Time? Resources? Connections? Those perceived advantages often dull us, making us lazy and rigid. Limited time and resources actually make us more creative as we look for means to accomplish the task that we may not have needed previously. It is said that necessity is the mother of all invention, and great leaders create a breeding ground for invention and re-imagination. Creating false deadlines or budgetary limits will ultimately increase urgency and productivity and reduce cost and error.

3. FORWARD FEEDBACK

Reward and punishment feedback systems are critical to reinforcing these ideas of false deadlines and budgets. When one trips over a buffered deadline but receives no consequence they are conditioned to believe that those deadlines don't really matter. When they are met either with reward or punishment the importance of that deadline is reinforced. This can be deployed both with teams and on an individual level. Rewards along the path are like the breadcrumbs on the trail, marking our way. Strategically placed rewards tied to accomplishing early deadlines and tight budgets reinforce those behaviors. I can hear you right

YOU WILL GET MORE OF WHAT YOU REWARD.

now saying "Ian, does it really make sense to reward people for what they're supposed to be doing anyways?" The answer, in this case, is unequivocally yes. Remember they're not being rewarded for what they should've been doing anyways, they're being rewarded for doing it faster and cheaper than it was required to be done. This creates compounding productivity. The organization wins and the team members win and you create a culture of getting things done in less time and at less cost. The time and money spent rewarding people who consistently deliver that result is one of the best investments your organization can ever make. Always remember you will get more of what you reward.

Entities and individuals benefit because the same task takes less time, and by default, costs less money. This creates room for secondary opportunities that could occupy the time and resources normally used to complete the first task. That is a win. On every level, that is a win. What could possibly be a better investment than rewarding the people who create these big wins after they've created them? It's a variable reward model where there's no reward paid unless the result is delivered early and under budget. The people who execute that task need to win as well.

In my private executive coaching practice, I work with some of the top corporate salespeople in the world whose incomes can be $700,000 or $800,000 a year, up to many millions of dollars annually. Almost always, the sales pros complain of being demoralized by ever-changing standards on which their compensation is set. They're not rewarded for consistently bringing home stellar results. They are expected to continue to bring more and more and more. Eventually, all of these pros leave for a better opportunity where their compensation isn't (at least, at first) tied to a never-ending sliding scale of performance. As a team, it could be as simple and inexpensive as recognizing them publicly, paying out a small bonus, or giving that team some extra time off. The reward needs to be commensurate with the value of the achievement. You can't give 10 employees a car for saving $5000 on a job, but there is no better way to create the behavior you want than by recognizing and celebrating it. On an individual level, strategically placed rewards and punishments offer course correction and pull us towards, or push us away from certain behavior patterns. You might be self-employed and have a productivity goal for work for the week. If you can hit that goal by Thursday maybe you leave early on Friday for some much-needed R&R. If you don't hit it by Thursday, maybe you come in for a half day Saturday. The reward pushes us towards accomplishing the task by Thursday and the punishment pushes us away from letting it slack, knowing we really have until Friday to get it done. Reward punishment plans are extremely effective when communicated clearly and thoroughly, upfront. The rules to the game, and that's what it is, a game, need to be known upfront and by all. What ends up happening when you successfully create a reward/punishment culture is you have made work, exercise, studying, and writing into a game. Almost always, people would rather play a game than work. When you make work a game, it's no longer work, it's fun and purpose-driven.

A caveat here is that the participants need to care about the reward and punishment. It needs to be something people value. Time, money, freedom, and significance are all good places to look when creating reward-punishment systems. and again it needs to be commensurate. You can't give mega incentives to people doing what they're supposed to be doing. Little wins equal small incentives, and big wins equal larger ones. For more on-reward punishment ideas, grab my book *BYPRODUCT* or grab the BYPRODUCT master class where we have an in-depth discussion about reward-punishment systems: what to use, when, and with who.

RUNNING UP THE SCORE

How good can you be? What record are you chasing? What game are you redefining? Teams and organizations that have a culture of urgency and focus are always playing for something. Think about somebody who redefined their niche: they reach previously unknown limits and then press them even further. How do they do it? What allows them to not be content at the very top but instead to own the very top, to make it synonymous with their name? Urgent organizations want to run up the score; they don't just want to win, they want to dominate their space.

They have an urgency to make something happen. Even when they may not see a way to make it happen there's still an urgency

HOW GOOD CAN YOU BE?

to make it happen. There's always a way and people with a sense of urgency find that way.

PLAYING UNDER PRESSURE

Pressure creates diamonds. It also breaks the weak. Pressure is what elevates us to our highest levels of achievement and simultaneously breaks us down to our lowest levels of training. Focused individuals and organizations learn to not only succeed under pressure, but to actually create it. They even go as far as to manifest and manufacture it as a tool in their arsenal of massive success. The people and teams who can deliver under pressure get all the goodies in life. Can you handle the pressure? Are you urgent? Do you have a singular focus on the task at hand? We live in a society where comfort is

CAN YOU HANDLE THE PRESSURE?

king. It's also where mediocrity breeds. Comfort and success are like oil and water, and if you want to do something big, you better get comfortable being uncomfortable. When the pressures are on, the greats turn up. The next time we feel the pressure of our dreams, the weight of our goals, and the urgency of our desires, remember to be grateful for those things because they are exactly what you need to get focused, dial in, and make things happen.

CHAPTER 13

FAITH

faith

/fāTH/

noun

1. complete trust or confidence in someone or something.

———

"Faith is the substance of things hoped for,
the evidence of things not seen"
(Heb. 11: 1, KJV).

F aith forges our resolve. It stirs us deeply when we are running on reserves. It pulls us toward our destiny. Let me make a bold statement here, we all have faith. The truth is, we all have faith in something. We all believe in some future outcome that has not happened yet. Faith is belief in a positive outcome. Doubt is faith in reverse. It's a belief in a negative outcome.

I recently spent some time in Key West with my family, and on our visit, we stopped by the Mel Fisher Maritime Museum, a staple of Key West history. Mel Fisher is one of the most famous treasure hunters in the world having recovered a Guinness World Record $400 million worth of treasure off the coast of Key West. What is interesting about Mel Fisher's story is his quest for the treasure of the Spanish ship Atocha is a story that spans the hundreds of years since the ship sank off the coast of Florida. For over 30 years, Mel Fisher went out every day in search of the storied treasure. Every day, as he would leave port, he would say, "Today is the day."[33]

Most people can't stay focused on something for three weeks, but for 30 years, Mel Fisher searched. He lost family members at sea, he was almost bankrupted multiple times, and for decades on end, he searched. There were times when nobody believed in him. Nobody but himself. It was his faith in the existence of the treasure and in his ability to find it that caused him to go on, day after day, for decades, until finally, one day, he pulled up one of the silver bars lost in the wreck.

Maybe you think, *What does faith have to do with business and self-development?* I believe it has everything to do with it. In this chapter, we are not talking about faith in the general sense of the term, as in faith in God, although, personally, I believe that it is instrumental to true and lasting success. For the purpose of our discussion here, we will take faith to mean the belief in an unseen future outcome. We all have faith; we all use faith every single day. When we get in our car to head to work or out on a family vacation, we don't truly know, with 100% certainty, that we will arrive at our destination. Every time we get on an airplane, we have no real guarantee. And that's life … no guarantees except death and taxes. Faith, our ability to trust and believe in certain, unseen outcomes, allows us to take the calculated, necessary risks to function in society. One commonality amongst all great leaders is that they have great faith, most in God yes, but also in their ability to shift the outcome. They have faith in cause and effect. They have faith in their ability to win, their ability to adapt, and their ability to change. When you believe in yourself, in your abilities, and in your commitment to winning, you are willing to make more accurate, bolder decisions. Why? Faith that it will work out because you are involved in it.

Many people, unsure of the potential outcome, choose not to act. They want to think about it, trying to get more and more information assembled to avoid making the wrong choice. While gathering intel is important, ultimately it's impossible to gather all the information needed to make most decisions because we simply can't tell the future. This is where faith becomes a liability or an asset. The higher level of faith you have in yourself, your teammates, your commitment, and your work ethic, the lower the amount of intel that must be gathered before making a decision and setting a course. Why? Because the details aren't important, you know whatever comes your way you will see it through. The lower the level of faith or the higher the level of doubt, the more information is required to make the DECISION. Faith reduces

THE GREATEST ACT OF FAITH IS PREPARATION.

our action threshold. The greatest act of faith is preparation. One of the greatest acts of preparation is preparing yourself mentally for the battle that lay ahead. If it were easy and predictable we wouldn't need faith. Faith is required because of the toughness that will be required from us.

MENTAL TOUGHNESS

In business and in life, it's not about talent, it's about toughness. Who has the grit and will to outlast, outmaneuver, and to out-deliver, over and over again? Great faith creates great mental toughness. Babe Ruth said, "It's hard to beat a person who never gives up."[34] Think about that for a second. Refusing to quit, doggedly attacking your goals relentlessly until they fall. There is not much that can withstand the weight of the human will. Virtually every major disease in human history has eventually succumbed to the power of the human collective against it. Act

WHAT'S IT GOING TO TAKE TO GET YOU TO GIVE UP

with enough controlled anger and direction against anything and eventually, it's going to fall. And that's what faith is about. It's about believing in the outcome so much it doesn't matter what obstacle is in the way. It is said that obstacles are what we see when we take our eyes off the prize. Faith is what allows us to see the prize in our minds and our hearts before we can see it with our eyes. Faith without toughness and tenacity is not faith at all, it's wishing.

What's it going to take to get you to give up and sell out on your dream? A promotion at work? A 10% pay raise? A critic? Somebody who thinks negatively about what you're doing? YOU ARE NOT FOR SALE. That's got to be your mindset all of the time. Your goals, your dreams, your

YOU ARE NOT FOR SALE.

passion, your calling; these are not for sale. There's no price on them because the price you would pay is giving up your dignity and destiny. When you're not for sale, you're different. Almost everybody has a price, but not you. The road to your goals has many clearly marked exits. They look like easier paths. They have rest stops and restaurants where all the sellouts eat. It takes toughness, specifically, mental toughness to endure the temptation to settle and make it into the promised land. As Sylvester Stallone famously said, "It's not about how hard you hit. It's about how hard you can get hit and keep moving forward. How much you can take and keep moving forward."[35] Life isn't going to give you what you want or would love to have, it's going to give you what you relentlessly fight for.

EARNED, NEVER GIVEN

Faith without works is dead. John Wooden's cornerstone of the pyramid of success is what he calls competitive greatness.[36] It's the love for the hard battle. Champions don't want something given to them. They want to earn it. The champion doesn't expect it to be easy, they expect it to be worth it. When you look back on Wooden's career it's easy in hindsight to see his greatness. The totality of his record reflects a championship coach … no question. But if you would have been a part of his first several seasons as he was building the framework of his later success you might have felt differently. Eight-plus years with no championships. Almost a decade in and even the most

> **THE CHAMPION DOESN'T EXPECT IT TO BE EASY, THEY EXPECT IT TO BE WORTH IT.**

committed and self-confident would begin to doubt. But not John Wooden. He was so sold out to his fundamentals approach to success that even after years of being denied a championship he still kept his relentless focus on building his team around the fundamentals. Faith is continuing to do the right things when the right results HAVEN'T shown up yet. It's about understanding the value of the work itself. It's about sacrificing now so that what you want doesn't become the sacrifice. The warrior who sweats more in training bleeds less in war. It's about facing adversities and setbacks and obstacles and exploding through them. Not just enduring them, but using them to become the fiercest competitor known to man.

Faith is about outlasting the competition. In every great battle, someone eventually gives up. That isn't going to be you. It's about standing and fighting instead of running from job to job, career to career relationship to relationship, and diet to diet. It's standing and fighting for what you want. Faith is about learning to see obstacles and adversities as opportunities instead of setbacks. They are tools to make you stronger and to give you the wisdom and execution that's only learnable by passing through the flames and living to tell about it. In the end, it's precisely what everyone else wishes they didn't have to go through that gives you the edge and keeps you on top!

Mental toughness is the clarity and strength of mind to persevere through obstacles and adversities in spite of how we feel. Feelings are liars. They change with the wind. Mental toughness is about being grounded in the truth. It's about accurate thinking. In this world, it's easy on the front end to follow the path of least resistance

FEELINGS ARE LIARS.

and create excuses. That path is easy, but the consequences are hard. Faith is about taking the road less traveled, following the truth no matter what the cost.

THIS BATTLE IN OUR BRAINS

Faith gives us the clarity of mind to look for, see, and pursue the solution instead of the temporary relief of quitting or backing off your goal. Most people when faced with disappointment, adversity, and obstacles quickly surrender their dreams and desires in a trade for temporary relief from the pain and pressure of persevering. They become confused, overwhelmed, distracted, and move into a state of short-term thinking. The mentally tough have a clear vision of the outcome that they seek. When circumstances don't line up with the reality in their mind, they aren't deterred. The greats have always done some level of reality-bending, shaping the world around them into the reality in their mind. Compare that to the path that most people take which is shaping their dream around today's reality. The average person fits their dreams into the box of their current situation no matter how small they have to be to make them fit. The greats bend reality to fit their dreams. In short, they find a way or they make one. When our faith is weak, when the vision of our future is opaque, we are subject to being carried away by the winds of adversity. Mentally tough people refuse to give up on what they want. Instead, they become incredibly resourceful and creative. Their vision is so strong it literally bends their wills and the circumstances around them. It's this refusal to quit that makes them unstoppable. The fact is that MOST PEOPLE QUIT. They quit school, marriages, jobs, friendships, social media, and church. PSA: Quitters quit! That's what they do. The problem with quitting is after the temporary relief, the problem is still there! Pain is temporary but quitting lasts a lifetime. Quitting on a worthwhile endeavor is never the answer. It's only after one refuses to quit that one effortfully releases its reward.

QUITTERS QUIT! THAT'S WHAT THEY DO.

FLIP THE SWITCH

Most of the battles we face are created by our own bad decision-making and short-term thinking. Mental toughness is about being willing to look at and learn these self-sabotaging tendencies and putting in safeguards against acting on them in the future. That's real leadership. Real toughness is the ability to know the darkest parts of yourself and keep yourself from acting on them, willing to look in the mirror and see the truth. It's seeing everything we are, everything we aren't, and what needs to be done to become who we are meant to be. Many prefer to hide behind titles, positions, and granted authority rather than having to look inward to see who they really are, and what they are really capable of. It's easier to hide behind the façade than to discover where our weaknesses lie

MOST OF THE BATTLES WE FACE ARE CREATED BY OUR OWN BAD DECISION-MAKING AND SHORT-TERM THINKING.

Mental toughness is where belief turns into action and you become an "in spite of" sort of person. Where you play through the pain towards a victory that is hard fought. The toughest battles create the sweetest victories. You must win in spite of the setbacks, you must win in spite of the money challenges, in spite of the health issues, in spite of the family drama, in spite of the haters, the negativity, and the overregulation. you've got to be a winning "in spite of it" sort of leader. When you're an "in spite of it" sort of person, it does not matter what presents itself, you're gonna find a way to win. When everybody's hitting the panic button, the "in spite of it" sort of leader is just digging in for the battle.

FAITH TO FIGHT

Sooner or later, you need to stand and fight or you will run the rest of your life—run from the discomfort, run from the call, and run from your destiny. Life isn't going to give you what you'd love to have, it's going to give you what you fight for. Stand up, declare war on average, break those chains holding you back, and walk into your destiny. It's about how much you can take, how bad you want it, and how bright that dream burns.

> **SOONER OR LATER, YOU NEED TO STAND AND FIGHT OR YOU WILL RUN THE REST OF YOUR LIFE**

HOW LONG CAN YOU STAND?

So much of winning is simply outlasting your competition, wanting it a little bit more, loving it a little bit more, and sacrificing for it just a little bit more. Everyone has a story, but no one cares about yours until you do something significant with it, until you outlast a significant struggle, and until you overcome insurmountable odds. So, when you're down to nothing, take heart, because God is up to something. From the deepest valleys come the greatest heights of achievement. When we observe a person exhibit extreme mental toughness, there's a piece of us that longs to be like that person. There's something inside of us, something primal, even instinctive, that knows it's our calling. That's our destiny, to be tough, to see it through, no matter what. And when we stand despite all odds, we unconsciously give others the courage to stand and fight their battles as well. Though you may be standing alone right now, people will thank you one day. They'll tell you, it's because of you, I didn't give up; it's because of you, I found the courage and the strength to fight my battles.

Our words matter, and these words, these 12 words, have made the difference in my life and in the lives of the people I've been honored to lead. If we're to become who we were meant to be, we must study these words, then act on them, and finally, embody them. It's time to live your message. It's time to let these words do a great work in you.

My hope and prayer for you is that one day, when you take your final breath, hopefully, surrounded by the people you love most, they will describe you with these 12 words. They will remember your positive attitude and how you always encouraged others. They will boast of your unwavering commitment to truth, your toughness, and your consistency. They will be inspired by your faith, built by your belief, and made courageous by the boldness of your action. Your desire for growth and relevance and your unwavering belief in yourself and the people around you will call them to stand taller and shine brighter. My prayer is that you live these words and that these words live out in you.

ENDNOTES

1. King, Martin Luther Jr. "I Have a Dream." Speech, Washington, D.C., August 28, 1963. American Rhetoric. http://www.americanrhetoric.com/speeches/mlkihaveadream.htm.

2. Roosevelt, Franklin D. " Day of Infamy." Speech, Washington, D.C., December 8, 1941. National Archives. https://www.loc.gov/resource/afc1986022.afc1986022_ms2201/?st=text.

3. Henry, Patrick. "Liberty or Death." Speech, Richmond, Virginia, March 23, 1775. Library of Congress. https://www.loc.gov/item/2001700209/.

4. Cleaver, Emanuel, U.S. Rep. "Opening Prayer." Speech, Kansas City, Missouri, January 25, 2021. US Congress. https://www.kansascity.com/news/local/news-columns-blogs/the-buzz/article248266055.html.

5. Kershner, Irvin. The Empire Strikes Back. 1980; Burbank, CA: Twentieth Century Fox Home Entertainment, 2006. DVD.

6. Prukner, Ian. *BYPRODUCT: Autonomous success in a bold new world.* United House Publishing, 2019.

7. Grover, Tim. *Relentless: From Good to Great to Unstoppable.* New York, NY, Scribner, 2013.

8. Oxford English Dictionary. 2nd ed. Oxford: Oxford University Press, 2004.

9. Vanderbilt University. "Undergraduate Honor Council." Vanderbilt University. Accessed April 29, 2023. https://studentorg.vanderbilt.edu/honorcouncil/honor-quotes/.

10. Merriam-Webster, s.v. "Relevance (n)," accessed May 20, 20223, https://www.merriam-webster.com/.

11. Merriam-Webster, s.v. "Belief (n)," accessed May 20, 20223, https://www.merriam-webster.com/.

12. Tassone, Samantha, Six Steps To Designing Thriving Relationship Connections In A Digital Social Exchange, Forbes, June 1, 2021, https://www.forbes.com/sites/forbescoachescouncil/2021/06/01/six-steps-to-designing-thriving-relationship-connections-in-a-digital-social-exchange/?sh=1c3036a14d75.

13. Ramsey, Dave. *The Dave Ramsey Show*. WWTN, Nashville, Tennessee, 1992.

14. Hall, Nancy. "Newton's Laws of Motion." National Aeronautics and Space Administration: Glenn Research Center. October 27, 2022. https://www1.grc.nasa.gov/beginners-guide-to-aeronautics/newtons-laws-of-motion/.

15. Personality Profile Solutions, LLC. "The DiSC Styles." DiSC Profile. 2023. https://www.discprofile.com/what-is-disc/disc-styles.

16. Williams, Art. "Just Do It." Speech, New York, New York, 1987, Art Williams Best. https://www.artwilliamsbest.com/.

17. Dalio, Ray. *Principles*. New York, New York: Avid Reader Press/Simon & Schuster, 2017.

18. Bjerke, Joshua. "American Workplace Study Finds Most Workers Lack Engagement with Their Jobs."Recruiter.com. Accessed April 28, 2023. https://www.recruiter.com/recruiting/american-workplace-study-finds-most-workers-lack-engagement-with-their-jobs/.

19. Anonymous. "A-Anonymous." Quotespedia. Accessed April 28, 2023. https://www.quotespedia.org/authors/a/anonymous/the-happiest-people-dont-

have-the-best-of-everything-they-just-make-the-best-of-everything-they-have-anonymous/#google_vignette.

20. Twain, Mark. "Quotable Quote," Goodreads, accessed April 29, 2023. https://www.goodreads.com/quotes/69056-i-can-teach-anybody-how-to-get-what-they-want.

21. Wooden, John. *They Call Me Coach.* New York City, New York, McGraw Hill, 2003.

22. *Cambridge University*, s.v. "consistency", May 10, 2023, https://dictionary.cambridge.org/dictionary/english/consistency.

23. Gillette, Hope. "How Long Does It Take to Form a Habit?" PsychCentral. March 6, 2023. Accessed May 10, 2023.

24. Dyer, Dr. Wayne W. *It's Never Crowded Along the Extra Mile.* Carlsbad, California: Hay House Publishing, 2002.

25. Forbes Media, LLC. "Forbes Quotes: Thoughts On The Business Of Life." 2015.

26. Gladwell, Malcolm. *Outliers: The Story of Success.* New York, New York: Back Bay Books, 2011.

27. Eisenhower, Dwight. 1954. "Address at the Second Assembly of the World Council of Churches." Transcript of speech delivered at Evanston, Illinois, August 19, 1954. presidency.ucsb.edu.

28. Keller, Gary. The ONE Thing: The Surprisingly Simple Truth About Extraordinary Results. Portland, Oregon: Bard Press, 2013.

29. Collins, Jim C. *Good to Great: Why Some Companies Make the Leap and Others Don't.* New York, New York: Harper Business Books, 2001.

30. Merriam-Webster, s.v. "law of diminishing returns (n.)," accessed May 14, 2023, https://www.merriam-webster.com/dictionary/law%20of%20diminishing%20returns.

31. Bob Carter, author

32. Plato. The Republic. Athens, Greece, 360 B.C.E. http://classics.mit.edu/Plato/republic.html.

33. Fisher, Mel & Tucker, Wendy. *Today's The Day!* The Mel Fisher Story. Manhattan, New York: Brick Tower Press, 2022.

34. Ruth, Babe % Luminary Group LLC. "Babe Ruth Quotes." 2023.

35. Stallone, Sylvester. *Rocky Balboa.* Culver City, California: Columbia Pictures, 2006, DVD.

36. Wooden, John. "The Pyramid of Success." The Wooden Effect. 1948. https://www.thewoodeneffect.com/pyramid-of-success/.

@IANPRUKNER

ABOUT THE AUTHOR

Ian Prukner was born and raised in Royal Oak, Michigan. As a child, he was taught to attend school, get good grades, and find a good job. At 23 years old, he found himself with a college degree, a new wife, and not one job, but three, trying to make ends meet. He describes himself during this time as dying inside as the real world took a toll on him, making only $27,000 a year and working 80-90 hours a week. He knew he wasn't happy or fulfilled, and deep down, he felt that there was something more for his life and his family. He would get up every day and drive past miles and miles of magnificent homes and say to himself, "There has got to be a better way." With every day that passed, he could feel his dreams slipping away. So, he decided to make a change. Less than ten years later, with no experience in business or sales of any sort, he found himself earning in excess of seven figures annually. His life was literally revolutionized, not just financially but in every area, including health and marriage relationship. He went from watching his dreams slip away to walking in them every single day. Today, he lives in his dream home, travels the world, and raises his three incredible kids with his wife. This book *BYPRODUCT* is itself, the byproduct of what he learned and applied over those 10 Years. It's what he used to drastically change everything in his life. It's a decade of leadership, learned in the trenches of American business, applied to life. This is how Ian did it.

Connect with Ian on Instagram: @ianprukner

FOLLOW @IANPRUKNER ON INSTAGRAM

RESOURCES

DiSC assessment: http://bit.ly/selfleadershipDISClinkorder

Connect with Ian: @ianprukner on Instagram

Contact Us: info@byproductbook.com

www.ingramcontent.com/pod-product-compliance
Lightning Source LLC
Chambersburg PA
CBHW071604210326
41597CB00019B/3392